Unshrink

MAX MCKEOWN AND PHILIP WHITELEY

Unshrink

Yourself ◦ Other People ◦ Business ◦ The World

An imprint of Pearson Education

London • New York • Toronto • Sydney • Tokyo • Singapore • Hong Kong • Cape Town
New Delhi • Madrid • Paris • Amsterdam • Munich • Milan • Stockholm

PEARSON EDUCATION LIMITED

Head Office:
Edinburgh Gate
Harlow CM20 2JE
Tel: +44 (0)1279 623623
Fax: +44 (0)1279 431059

London Office:
128 Long Acre
London WC2E 9AN
Tel: +44 (0)20 7447 2000
Fax: +44 (0)20 7447 2170
Websites: www.business-minds.com
          www.yourmomentum.com

First published in Great Britain in 2002

The right of Max McKeown and Philip Whiteley to be identified
as Authors of this Work has been asserted by them in accordance
with the Copyright, Designs and Patents Act 1988.

Unshrink is a trademark.

ISBN 0 273 65614 7

British Library Cataloguing in Publication Data
A CIP catalogue record for this book can be obtained from the British Library

10 9 8 7 6 5 4 3

Designed by Claire Brodmann Book Designs, Lichfield, Staffs.
Typeset by Northern Phototypesetting Co. Ltd, Bolton
Printed and bound in Great Britain by Bookcraft, Midsomer Norton

The Publishers' policy is to use paper manufactured from sustainable forests.

Unshrink

- **To restore to original amount or value**
  Her potential was much greater once it had been unshrunk.

- **To choose radical solutions without starting all over again**
  Society must change from where it is – it must be unshrunk

- **To have fun or be kind when there is no reason not to**
  I had an unshrink moment today when my son wanted to ride to school on his mini scooter and I said yes

- **To cause to unshrink**

Contents

Myths

- ◄ You are what you do

- ◄ Work comes first

- ◄ The boss is superhuman

- ◄ The plan must be secret

- ◄ People obey orders

- ◄ Organizations are machines

- ◄ All change is good

Principles

▶ You are what you can become

▶ Life always comes first

▶ We are all human

▶ Only the goal unifies

▶ Only good change is good

▶ The organization is a community

▶ People do what they want

There's a lot to unshrink

This is a message.

'We are condemned to choose', wrote Jean-Paul Sartre. To choose, however, one needs a rationale. Perfect knowledge of information is rare, so our reasons for exercising a certain choice involve faith. We are condemned to believe. But to believe in what?

In this slim volume, we will argue that our beliefs have shrunk us. We have been shrunk. Bad news isn't it? The potential that we had at the start has been diminished. We and our world are less than we should be.

We are astonishingly intelligent. Our genius is not new and is not confined to an elite. It can be seen in the ghetto and in the boardroom. We are also curiously prone to superstition. The scientist designs a space rocket but knocks on wood before the flight, just to be sure.[1] We are interdependent. Our modern world cannot function without the assistance of others.

This is our human species then: intelligent, superstitious and dependent upon one another. So why do we demean and compete against each other? Why do our economic theories portray us as either coldly rational or stupid? Why do we suffer depression and stress in silence? Why do we display indifference towards 'them' and illogical loyalty towards 'us'?

Our shrinking myths tell us that we are what we do, that work is more important than life, that capital creates value, that people are stupid, that people do as they are told, that all change is good, that plans must be kept secret and that the organization is a machine.

These myths cause good people to do harmful things. In this book, we will meet the sports coach who thinks that leadership means shouting, the companies that think that long hours boost profits and the campaigners who think that to give to some you must steal from others. No research, no logic supports these approaches. We have assembled a case that demonstrates the opposite – that virtue is the friend of success.

> **These myths cause good people to do harmful things.**

Why do such myths retain their force? Typically, they are presented as 'authoritative and factual no matter how much they are at variance with natural law of ordinary experience'. And are generally only obvious from the distance of another society, time or, occasionally, from outside individual businesses or relationships. Distance gives us clarity that is not enjoyed by those close to the problem. Dominant myths are rarely questioned for the simple reason that they are accepted as true and are not debated since they are assumed to be factual and *'just the way that things are'*.

Myth has existed in every society. Indeed, it would seem to be a basic constituent of human culture. Because the variety is so great, it is difficult to generalize about its nature. But it is clear that in both general characteristics and details myths reflect, express and explore people's self-image.

Myths try to present themselves as factual by offering as many details as they can. With myths of heroes, this might mean details of geography and genealogy. With economic myths, this means giving examples or even contorted research that adds weight to a belief that is widely held. Additional etiological explanations and theories are built on a mythical foundation that becomes accepted as equally valid as the myth. The questionable assumption becomes accepted as fact through nothing other than repetition, and an entire industry, is built around it. *Voilà* – business books.

Within the same country, political party, business or team, there may be competing, conflicting myths that distort reality differently for those who believe them. Attempts at improving our organizations or our societies will struggle unless they are based on reality rather than on myths.

These beliefs blind business and individuals to the source of real value. One researcher suggests that businesses are up to 85 per cent blind because they cannot account for 85 per cent of their value using traditional valuation methods. We think it's even worse because they cannot see the link between society, individuals and their own businesses.

Value creation cannot stand on its on. It is linked to the world. It satisfies a need or it has no value. So what needs do we want it to satisfy? We start to believe that this is just the way things are. That the value is created by capital, not people! Or that the market gives us unerringly what we want, while wondering why we so rarely have what we are really looking for.

This book makes a bold claim. It seeks to identify, expose, defog and debunk the shrinking myths that educate the way that work is carried out and managed in our world and reduce the world's capacity to serve its inhabitants. The study of myths provides insights into the true nature of human society and the study of the shrinking myths will provide insights into the true nature of work and its place in life.

To replace the myths we will need new principles to give us back our sleep, mutual respect and self-worth while at the same time increasing passion and profitability. These principles will help us deal with our world, our ever more complex world, the way it is.[2] We argue that clear principles and truths help us understand unclear events and situations.

Being all knowing is not a human quality.

What is the alternative? We don't have brain capacity to deal with all of creation at once. Being all knowing is not a human quality. Omniscience is not yet part of our genetic legacy. So, what we have to do is use principles to view the world and make sense of its complexity piece by little piece.

We need the principles to be true so that they can provide a foundation for future action and understanding. We also need them to be easy to remember or we will forget them. It must finally be possible to apply them to the smallest and to the largest of issues. Principles can be 'one size fits all' in a way that rules cannot. If we live by true principles then we can govern ourselves (and so can those who work for us, with us and around us).

From these principles we discover that we are not what we do, but what we can become. That work does not come first, it should only serve life. That we are all are human – boss and employee alike. That the plan must stop being secret so that it can unify everyone. That only good change is good. That our organizations and our world are communities not machines. That they are only improved as we share. And that sharing will only happen as trust is built *not* as the number of rules is increased.

Does this mean anarchy? Far from it. But it does mean not treating employees like criminals, sheep, rats, half-wits or naughty children. It means a workplace for grown-up, complete people with families, brains, unfulfilled ambitions and pride. People who will follow willingly when they understand the principles, believe in them and are permitted the freedom to follow their own initiative in so doing.

Animals do not provide a whole lot of instruction for the manager despite the best attempts of some psycho-, anthro- and zoo-ologists to apply their lab and field findings to modern organizations. We expect (and rely upon) a person to keep working creatively and competently when we are not there to watch over them. We do not expect the same of a dog, horse, cow, sheep, bird or rat. Do we?!

Despite our admiration for a well-trained sheep dog, it will not herd sheep into holding pens while the farmer drives to an appointment with an accountant. The comparisons all mark out homo sapiens as so different from their animal buddies that it should merely remind us how differently they need to be treated if we want to benefit from their vast store of abilities.

And that is where our new word comes in. Unshrink, simply defined, is to restore something to its natural dimensions. It leads to radical change *without* going back to the beginning.

Unshrinking is different from growing potential because we believe that people are stopped from reaching their natural stature and ability. People don't have to be forced to grow. Growth is not the gift of educators, managers, social workers and politicians. It is innate and vigorous at birth. The trouble is what happens between birth and death. So often, lives can be termed the shrinking years.

Unshrink, simply defined, is to restore something to its natural dimensions.

Unshrinking yourself is the starting point because we need to know how amazing we are and what we need in order to be fulfilled before we will start doing it. We start to unshrink others because it's the most effective way of unshrinking ourselves. We start to unshrink business because that's where most of us spend most of our time. And then we focus those unshrunk businesses on unshrinking the world.

This is based on the age-old wisdom of the second commandment *and* the golden rule taught by all the world's main faiths. From Buddhism we learn to 'hurt not others in ways that you yourself would find hurtful', and from Confucianism that the 'maxim of loving-kindness should be acted upon throughout one's whole life'. Hinduism teaches us that 'the sum of duty is to do nothing unto others which would cause you pain if done to you', while Islam makes it clear that 'no one is a believer until he desires for others what he desires for himself'. Judaism is equally clear that the entire law states that 'what is hateful to you, do not to your fellow men', and Christianity that 'All things whatsoever ye would that men should do to you, do ye even so to them'.

It is in unshrinking individuals that we will increase nations' prosperity or improve the world's situation. To let everyone know who they are and what they can be. We believe too readily that progress requires a 'dog eat dog' world and dismiss the truth in other pieces of similarly clichéd phrases such as 'every dog has his day' or the simple idea that the 'pack needs every dog'. It wouldn't be much of a pack without them would it?

If it is against these principles, if it is against moral principles, it will not be right even if someone tells you that it will work! Even if it appears to work in the shorter term, you should be prepared to look deeper and understand what is really going on. Principles prepare you for the future because they let you make a choice before you see the results and it is too late to reverse a disaster.

Principles prepare you for the future.

Consider the infamous Al 'Chainsaw' Dunlap, the former chief executive of North American electrical goods supplier Sunbeam, who delighted naïve investors by waging war with his own employees in the mid-1990s. He claimed that he was improving the products by cutting staff, but he cut so many people that he couldn't even get the company's products out to its customers. No products, no revenue. No revenue, eventually meant no Al, but only after thousands had lost their jobs at the company that he had led, which came close to liquidation after two years of Dunlap's policies.[3] No anti-globalisation demonstrators could have wreaked so much damage to a capitalist organisation in such a short period of time.

No one dared to say anything, or he wouldn't believe them when they spoke, or everyone who he listened to told him what he wanted to hear. He wanted higher returns so he did what the market tends to like – which is to be a macho, job-cutting manager. His views were clear from the start:

❝I take a very dim view of [the idea of stakeholders]. In the first place, business is not a social experiment. Business is a very serious undertaking. I believe the shareholders own the corporation.❞

Unfortunately, the extremely bad, nonsensically bad, management of someone like Chainsaw Al, who rejoiced in calling himself 'Rambo in Pinstripes', draws attention away from the slightly less bad management of other businesses. His failure allows poorly managed competitors to survive, just as the failure of absurd national policies allows wasteful governments to survive. The status quo unchallenged.

The first thing that we have to remember is that the good guys need to win – it makes the world better. The other point is that truly good guys are more likely to succeed than others. (We invite you to wait until the end of the book before deciding if you disagree.)

Don't make the mistake of thinking that stating our views with verve means that we are less well researched than other writers. If it hurts your brain and forces you to think then we will have already achieved more than the average MBA.

Time to dig deeper.

1

Unshrink yourself

Have you ever felt small? Have you ever felt dead inside? Have you wanted the world to swallow you? Have you wanted to disappear – to just fade away? Have you considered being a hero? Do you want to be better than you are? Have you ever considered yourself a failure? Do you feel that you have weaknesses? Do you think that you can do anything about them?

It all starts as we are born. There is a hole, a role, a space, a shape, a label ready for us into which we must squeeze, distorting our natural shape, restricting our innate potential, limiting and damaging who we are, how we think, what we can become.

What we can be pretty sure of is that we have already developed certain aspects of ourselves more than others. Specialization occurs not only when we adopt certain careers but is a common aspect of our lives. Genetically we find certain behaviours and tasks easier than others from, and before, birth. Our carers, peers, siblings and teachers will also play a significant part in 'shaping us' – directing us towards what they find interesting or valuable themselves *or* what they feel that you will be best at *or* what they feel is least threatening to themselves.

The young Pip, in Charles Dickens' *Great Expectations*, observed: 'Everyone acted as though I had absolutely insisted upon being born.'

Who should you listen to? How do you choose? The person with the best qualifications? The one with your interest at heart? The one with experiences that match your own? Who should be the most responsible for your welfare? Who should be the greatest expert on you? How do you get rid of others' opinions, comments and actions that have shrunk you in some aspect of your life? Whom should you trust? Should you trust anyone at all?[1]

We start to ask many of these questions during adolescence. Before then we tend to accept what we are told. This state of acceptance can be helpful in preparing us for adult life. There is very useful information about our world that our carers are meant to pass on to us. This includes the vital, 'don't put your hand in fire' warning from which we learn that we are not fire-proof and can avoid pain and injury.

Unfortunately, this same state of acceptance (or innocence) can lead us to believe what just isn't accurate or healthy about our world and ourselves. We tend to accept limits that are just not acute. As children, we will believe a carer who tells us that we are

There is more to you than you know.

smart, dumb, fat, thin, clumsy, agile, useful, useless, greedy, self-less, or any other label that they wish to bestow upon us. We develop internal voices, which may be affirming, such as 'I'm gifted at music' or 'It is good to help others'. But some voices shrink us: 'I'm stupid; others know more than me' or encourage us to shrink others 'I can do what I want and it doesn't matter'.

Because we don't know who we are yet, we can start to believe that we are what we do. We are our jobs. We are our mistakes. We are our education. We are our qualifications. We are our prizes – or lack of them. We are our ability to tell jokes, sing or dance. And, since when we are born we have done nothing, sometimes we are treated as though that is what we are.

There is more to you than you know. More to me than I know. Isn't that exciting? Neither of us knows what the other will become. Neither of us knows exactly how smart, dedicated, loyal, funny, original, kind, strong or wise we are.

MYTH YOU ARE WHAT YOU DO

Do you believe that this myth is true? Do you want to be reduced to fit a job description? Why is it that we ask what a stranger does before we ask what kind of person they are or what they are interested in?

Even kind, well-meaning carers can shrink our self-expectations. They base what they explain to us on what they have experienced themselves, including their childhood. They may not think it is possible for a child to become a complete person. They may have assumed that people are either 'one thing' or 'another' with no room for complete development.

We do not mean to add to the weight of guilt on the shoulders of modern parents. Our aim is a different one: to discuss how, in our compartmentalized, Western thinking, we often look at roles, not people; at limits, not potential. It is a difficult balance, because we know that some parents encourage their children to seek their potential in an aggressive way; to believe that they can do what they want; to win at all costs. There are a few aggressors and many timid individuals frightened to step out of line and believing that they must lose their soul if they seek advancement. Neither extreme is healthy. This book will challenge the view that success comes at the expense of others. There is more than one way to succeed. To win at all costs damages yourself as well as others and, because of the distortions to your soul and the resentment created in others, it is less sustainable.

It is a wonderful thing to become the world's greatest anything, but not at the cost of your humanity. If all aspects of human development were equally respected and valued then fewer people would experience such distorted, shrunken, incomplete personalities, lives, abilities and characters.

What happens when any single characteristic, including physical prowess, is singled out as the most important aspect of an individual's life and development? What are the dangers of a person accepting the lie that the ability to throw a ball, swing a bat, or lift heavy objects is more important than honesty, relationships, education or patience?

Athletes become convinced that the 'being on the team' and 'being the best' are more important than other more pedestrian considerations of 'being healthy' and 'being happy'. It is not a new problem. The first competitors were disqualified from the Olympics for 'ingesting mushrooms and animal protein' in 300BC.[2] With the belief 'you are what you do', the task is elevated above the character; the end above the means. It can lead to a more dangerous assumption that 'winning at all costs' is what matters.

'Winning at all costs' is a phrase that can blind participants to what the costs really are. It hints that winning a particular prize requires ruthlessness and the sacrifice of all other valuable rewards; that one must trample on others to succeed. In this book we will offer many examples of how that is not so.

This attitude infects business to the detriment of individuals, families and society. Take an advert for a sales person for Novastar Corporation, a provider of technology based in California, that insists candidates have 'the attitude to win at all costs'.[3] This expectation leads to debilitating job pressure, the breaking of laws and the sacrifice of life upon the altar of sales targets.

'Winning at all costs' is a phrase that can blind participants to what the costs really are.

By contrast, SAS Institute, based in North Carolina, USA, declares: 'The best way to produce the best and get the best results is to behave as if the people who are creating those things for you are important to you. It just means that you take care of the folks who are taking care of you.'[4] Its employees work only 35 hours a week. It is phenomenally successful.

The same pattern appears to be occurring in crime enforcement where illegal actions are taken to catch those who may or may not have committed illegal actions! In examples documented by investigative reporters[5] some law enforcement agencies in the USA appear to have adopted a philosophy that, 'whatever works is what's right'[6] This leads to intimidation of suspects, brutality, fabrication of evidence and the conviction of the innocent. Those who contribute to the pressure and look the other way forget what the real objective is.

Clarisse Machanguana, professional basketball player in the US-based Women's National Basketball Association, questions the 'win at all costs' ideas that are accepted so often. She lists a number of incidents to illustrate her concern:

- a professional baseball coach who lied to his players about everything, including being in Vietnam, in order to motivate his players to win using any means necessary;[7]

- the father of a hockey player who killed another man in a dispute over a game in front of his only son and the three children of the murdered man;

- a player who violently elbowed a star member of the opposition, causing temporary blindness, because he was told by his coach that they could not win unless that particular player was removed from the game.

Clarisse Machanguana concluded:

"I think that this eagerness to win at all times and at all costs is getting out of control, both within the context of sports and in real life issues in general. I think we have taught ourselves that winning is the only thing that matters and all else that is experienced while pursuing the goal of winning is irrelevant. A kid who tries his best to win and doesn't is most likely to be hassled, labelled as a loser and thus feel like a loser."

Bob Knight was coach of the Indian University basketball team for 25 years. During this time he verbally and physically abused his players but many people, such as the following journalist, found ways of justifying his behaviour:

> **"**No, I've never hit a Puerto Rican policeman before practice at the Pan-American games; stuffed a fan from an opposing team in a garbage can; told Connie Chung, 'I think that if rape is inevitable, relax and enjoy it'; told women, 'There's only two things you people are good for: having babies and frying bacon'; pretended to bullwhip my star player; waved used toilet paper in my players' faces to provide them with a metaphor for their poor play; tossed a chair across the court during a game; kicked my son — a player on the team — in the leg during another game; head-butted a player during yet another game; or choked another player during practice. **But** neither have I won three NCAA championships, twice been named coach of the year, coached the United States to an Olympic gold medal, won more than 700 college basketball games or had a higher graduation rate among my players than nearly any other Division I basketball coach.**"** [8]

Listen to the recordings of Bob Knight instructing his players and you can understand why so many transferred away from the school.[9] Listen to them again and it is clear that he is an example of the kind of deformed personality that occurs when success is seen as synonymous with cruelty and inhumanity. As long as this lie is told and believed, we will have managers, leaders and individuals like, and worse than, Bob Knight.

Sometimes behaviour is excused because it is thought to be part of the toughness that is necessary to win, rather than the actions of men who know that they can get away with anything, who could have been nice *and* still been successful. If someone succeeds, not everything they did contributed to that success.

The idea that each great man or woman must have a great, and awful, fault that will lead ultimately to their demise is false. It is also permission for each man or woman who aspires to greatness to let their weaknesses loose, rampant upon the world that will justify and accept such flaws as part of the territory of genius. The fatal flaw is not our fate! We have weaknesses but we have the means to overcome them.

We have weaknesses but we have the means to overcome them.

Leaders achieve greatness despite their faults, not because of them, and certainly not due to any bullying tendencies. Research shows that coercion can only be effective in certain circumstances – over short timescales – and even then it relies upon people finding motivation from somewhere.[10] In the next chapter, when we discuss leadership, we will look at some inspiring examples of humane leadership, including one from the world of sport. The highest results are achieved, but in a manner that is sustained because it makes people feel good about themselves.

'I think you do everything you can to win, but you do it within a certain set of rules. To win at all costs, that's tragic,' said American footballer Troy Aikman, drawing applause from a crowd of newspaper executives.[11] He appeared to understand that not only will such an approach often lead to personal tragedy, it will also not necessarily lead to the greatest financial or career success.

Were there any influencers in this balanced, unshrunk approach? It's worth noting that as a child, sometimes Troy Aikman's confidence spilled over into unsporting behaviour as when, at eight years old, he screamed at his baseball coach when he was replaced by another child that *'this kid was no good and should not be in the game'*. Troy eventually played and even helped save the game but his mother did not congratulate him at first but instead 'chewed him out' for being 'so ugly on the field'. It's a clear example of a guide making clear the importance of many different kinds of achievement.

Did Troy Aikman become a soft-hearted loser? Nope. In fact he is the only quarterback in history to win three Super Bowl titles in only four years. He has become a 'soft-hearted winner', setting up a series of projects that help children including a foundation that benefits children's charities, an area in a hospital where critically ill children can escape their illnesses through play, an interactive site on the internet designed for critically ill children, and published his autobiography of which all proceeds go to charity.

So what could stop you being successful? What is success? How do you know when you have been successful?

The easiest route is to be born to good parents who give you an unshrinking environment, free of unhelpful labels and prejudice, full of stimulus, education, truth and belief. We did not choose our birth environment, but most of us were fortunate to have some of these healthy ingredients. We have much to build on.

If you can read this book then you can start to unshrink yourself. You are capable of accepting that responsibility and life's work.

You can begin to unpack the potential that has been packed so tightly into the space you have had to develop.

We all need room to unshrink. We need room in our personal lives, in our professional lives, in our homes and in our heads. With that room we can rediscover our real identity and what we really want to achieve.

We need not only friends but supporters, allies and believers in us and our potential.

We need not only friends but supporters, allies and believers in us and our potential. Their belief provides us with the room our minds need to work harder, do more, experiment with the new and untried, take risks, heal wounds and unshrink.

Everyone starts from an unproven position. Everyone needs to be given a chance to prove him or herself. You need to grab hold of people who will give you that chance. You need to pull them into your corner. And first you need to make sure you are in the right corner of the ring and that you are fighting for your own cause. For the whole person you can be.

Everyone who ever achieved anything had to start from somewhere. Stephen King did not begin life with an adoring fan base but he did begin life with the ability to become a successful novelist. He had that inside him all his life.

Not everyone appreciated that in Stephen King's childhood. His grandfather once said to his mother: *'Why don't you shut that boy up, Ruth? When Stephen opens his mouth, all his guts fall out!'* But King's wife, Tabby, did see it. She pulled his first manuscript out of the bin after it had been discarded. They were living in a caravan, car not working, telephone disconnected and she still believed in him. He didn't need an office of his own or a secretary to be able to write a book. He needed her support, her belief. He explains:

> **❝My wife made a crucial difference during those two years ... If she had suggested that the time I spent writing stories was wasted, I think that a lot of the heart would have gone out of me. Tabby never voiced a single doubt ... Writing is a lonely job. Having someone who believes in you makes all the difference. They don't have to make speeches. Just believing is usually enough.❞** [12]

So much of our life's efforts can be lonely. We can live in the room provided for us by the belief of others – in their minds and hearts. The book that Tabby retrieved from the waste paper bin eventually sold in 1974 for $400,000. I am not sure that the money matters, but it should be remembered that the belief came before effort and that the effort came before the sale. Which brings us to our first principle.

PRINCIPLE 1 YOU ARE WHAT YOU CAN BECOME

We recently read a book called *Smart Luck* (Andrew Davidson: Pearson, 2001) to look at the life histories of some entrepreneurs. It was notable that a lot of them were near the top or the bottom of what we would call our class hierarchy and our class culture (if we had one!). One example was Simon Woodruff, who launched a chain of sushi bars in London. During an interview, Woodruff said something really interesting. The journalist conducting the interview described how Woodruff had launched his business, been in the press a lot, and had written a book called *The Story of Yo!*, about his very limited business career to date. Then the journalist asked 'But then you stopped, why did you stop?'

(Just as a reminder, it's a bad thing if he stops. It doesn't create any wealth. If he stops, someone else gets the wealth.)

So what did Woodruff say? He said: 'It was a confidence thing. I lost my confidence.'

> **To be a success at being an entrepreneur (or anything else) is really a confidence class thing.**

He was afraid that it wouldn't last, that it couldn't last. He simply had no experience with success. No peer group with victory assumptions to strengthen him.

So one of the important things is that it's not about being upper class or middle class; to be a success at being an entrepreneur (or anything else) is really a confidence class thing. That's what we need to do – give people the confidence to do more and be more; give each other confidence. Understand that there is a world outside your mind that will bring you answers, comfort and a full night's sleep. Even where involvement with it will challenge your ideas and your life style, it will reward you with more than it will cost.

When you shed the debilitating myths that hold you back; defeat the internal voices telling you that 'you're no good' or 'others know more than you', a most inspiring transformation takes place. You grow in confidence and self-awareness, and the people around you grow also. But something else, something quite extraordinary, starts to happen: you start to achieve more than you thought you ever could. You do 'better than your best'. That sounds like a contradiction, but it actually happens. Musicians, for example, will say to themselves, when they hear a recording of their finest work, 'Is that really me? It cannot be; I am not good enough to play that!'

Try believing the way that the singer, India Arie does: 'When I look in the mirror the only one there is me. Every freckle on my face is where it's supposed to be. And I know our creator didn't make no mistakes on me. My feet, my thighs, my lips, my eyes – I'm lovin' what I see.'

Provided we avoid the temptations of vanity we can keep on unshrinking. Our limits are unknowable, so the saddest thing is when we never seek to explore them and discover truly what we can do. This is not just for work and careers: it is for child-rearing, for relationships, for our interests, for our life.

The best leaders encourage us to view a failure as a temporary setback, not a symptom of a character flaw. The bully does the opposite, telling us 'Of course you failed; what did you expect?' Our argument is that the damaging beliefs that we have identified encourage good people to become bullies.

The idea that each great man or woman must have a great, and awful, fault that will lead ultimately to their demise is false. It is also permission for each man or woman who aspires to greatness to let their weaknesses loose, rampant upon the world that will justify and accept such flaws as part of the territory of genius. The fatal flaw is not our fate! We have weaknesses but we have the means to overcome them.

Some bully because they grew up in a violent environment, some because they were encouraged to get their own way, but others bully because their management training or the culture of their industry or sport has taught them, very, very subtly, that junior people are stupid and that demeaning them improves results. This we shall discuss more in Chapter 3.

The idea that you cannot alter your world or yourself is the most wasteful, tragic idea.

Let's look at some of the forces that can contribute to us being less than we could be. First up is, fatalism: the acceptance of things the way they are and you the way you are because it's just the way it is or just the way that some force or other wills it to be. The idea that you cannot alter your world or yourself is the most wasteful, tragic idea. It prevents each of us from being more and it prevents the world from reinventing itself.

Fatalism is a contributor to apathy and inactions. It is also an enemy to freedom of thought. It prevents us getting out of the dead ends in our heads and seeing the big picture for what it really is. It encourages us to accept limitations, including those handed out in the form of discrimination, racism and prejudice.

Consider Marilyn Monroe who, speaking of her childhood, said:

❝I was never used to being happy, so that wasn't something I ever took for granted. You see, I was brought up differently from the average American child because the average child is brought up expecting to be happy.❞

As a little girl she was told that she 'was a mistake' but never that she 'was pretty'. As a result, Marilyn Monroe simply did not expect to be happy and she carried this shrunken, reduced expectation of life into adulthood.

She made an immense effort to find herself in a Hollywood system that 'only cared about money' where 'you're judged by how you look, not by what you are'. She said of herself that: 'To put it bluntly, I seem to have a whole superstructure with no foundation. But I'm working on the foundation.' After all the money, the marriages and the movies she concluded:

❝I'm trying to find myself as a person, sometimes that's not easy to do. Millions of people live their entire lives without finding themselves. But it is something I must do.❞

Compare her with a doctor in a desperately poor neighbourhood in Managua, Nicaragua. Her surgery is a run-down, single-storey building in a battered terrace of houses, a couple of blocks from a huge waste tip where dozens of families scavenge items amid swarming vultures. She pulls up in her rickety, battered car. She is young, animated and intelligent, with eyes that dart about and glow with enthusiasm. She talks about her work tending to some very poor families, where basic nutrition is as much a medical need as anything else. She talks about the difficulties of obtaining medicines on a basic budget, of having enough time to see people. It is difficult to refer patients to hospitals as they are full of people wounded from the war. She describes her weekly clinic with the children of the neighbourhood, commenting at the end that it is challenging. But then, completely unprompted, just at the point where one expects a weary sigh, her eyes light up into a glow. She cannot help it. A smile breaks out on her face as she adds: 'Pero es *lindo* trabajo con los niños!' (It is *lovely* work with the children!). She speaks with passion, joyously pro-

> **Human potential is NOT fixed. Over time it may well be infinite.**

longing the word 'l-i-i-ndo' in the way that happy Latin Americans do. There is no one in the world more fulfilled in her work.[13]

We do not wish to idealize her challenges, nor excuse the poverty. The point is to expose the myth that the key to one's fulfilment lies entirely outside oneself, in fate or in the environment. She is unshrunk in the ghetto and Marilyn Monroe was shrunken in Hollywood. People caught up in a genuine tragedy, such as destitution or a civil war, often spend little time bemoaning their luck. Some of them cross oceans, start a new life and end up running a successful business. Or they tend to the sick, bring up a family and preserve some joy and hope for the next generation.

Human potential is NOT fixed. Over time it may well be infinite. And even over the limited period of a single human lifetime it is considerable.

Even your brain cells are capable of regeneration, depending on how much they are used.[14] The neurons, hippocampus, branches, cerebral cortex and synapses that contain your memories and your ability to process information, innovate, dream and experience can all be enhanced and repaired. Depression, stress, guilt and poor self-image all reduce your brain's performance while caring, working, loving, relaxing, playing and meditating all increase it.

You can start smart and end dumb, or start dumb and end smart. Up to a 60 per cent difference each year depending on what you choose to do with your potential. What an idea! Given the right kinds of effort (mental, emotional and physical) you can unshrink your brain – think of the possibilities and by the end of this book you may actually be more intelligent.[15]

But what kind of intelligence will you have gained? What kind of intelligence do you want? IQ is just a measure of a particular kind of efficiency in brain design. That's important for doing IQ-type tasks but what happens when you want to complete a task that IQ doesn't measure?

Howard Gardener is among many who have examined what he termed 'multiple intelligence'. His first attempt identified six 'intelligences' that contribute to our society's success:

- musical
- logical
- spatial
- bodily

- interpersonal and
- intrapersonal.

He later added naturalistic, which is the ability to recognise and classify objects in the environment that in adults might mean plants, minerals and animals but in children might start with the ability to identify cultural artefacts like cars and sneakers. Not the kind of thing that IQ (and IQ-based aptitude tests) value at all, with damaging impacts on the way that people are valued , as in the following example:

> **"I feel as if I've been shrunk down to pea size by an experience I had last week whilst filling in an on-line application form for a job. I got to the section where it wanted to know how I did at high school but I thought this was OK as I think I have proved my abilities in my university years. So, I type 14, my number of UCAS points (gained through the UK examination system) into the required box. The next thing I know I am taken to a page that read: 'Sorry, you do not meet our entry requirements. Your application has been unsuccessful.' I had been shrunk to the number 14."**

What do you expect from those whom you work with or from those who work for you? That includes students for teachers, teachers for students, employers for employees, employees for employers, men for women, women for men, parents for their children, and children for their parents. In a way that we cannot perhaps entirely explain, the belief of another person changes what they do for us *and* what we will do from that point on.

When you see no hope of improvement, will you intervene to help that person or that situation improve? Nine times out of ten, you will not. The average person would not try to achieve something they thought was unachievable. But how do they decide what is possible and what is not? We ask ourselves whether anyone else has ever done it, whether anyone else thinks we can do it, whether we are getting the help we need to do the impossible.

The average person would not try to achieve something they thought was unachievable.

When we divide the world into successes and failures – those who can and those who never will – we stop working for the good of those supposedly 'hopeless cases'. Teachers have been found to 'cling to the belief that some students cannot learn', while others 'with high expectations for all students, on the other hand, effectively translate their beliefs into more academically demanding curriculum'.[17]

Has this ever happened to you? Did anyone ever decide that you couldn't do something and so reduce the teaching and the opportunities that were given to you? Have you ever made that decision for someone else? It can happen through racial stereotyping, with black children encouraged to do sport and music when they might rather do law or medicine. Every time it happens someone shrinks. They could have done more but now they might not.

What value could you see in the paralysed ninth child of 22 siblings? Or in a boy whose childhood home was a hut with walls smoothed with cow dung in the African village of Qunu? Or in a poor, sexually abused, black girl who was pregnant at 14 years old? Or in a man who could only communicate by raising his eyebrows?

How about a gifted poet and artist? How about the leader who reversed the cultural and political structure of an entire country? How about the media phenomenon with an estimated personal fortune of more than $500 million? How about the esteemed academic and author of the best selling *A Brief History of Time*?

Dyslexia has continued to be allowed to shrink those with the condition. Study after study has shown that if teachers lower their expectations for students with dyslexia they leave school with poor reading and writing skills. They are penalized in the workplace, suffer from the symptoms of shrunken self-confidence, and are more likely to experience failure and frustration in all areas of their lives.

The prison population is 50 per cent more likely to be dyslexic than the general population. Some 85 per cent of those who are illiterate have dyslexia.[18] And yet that dyslexic student may become the next Woodrow Wilson, Thomas Edison or Albert Einstein! You don't know who you are teaching, interviewing or managing until you have seen all that they can become.

When we consider how many kinds of intelligence we need, and how people each have different combinations, we can start to value supposed 'disabilities' and 'limitations' differently. We know that the average dyslexic person is more creative, the average blind person better at listening, and a deaf person better with visual perception. Should dyslexia, blindness, deafness and other 'disabilities' become positive qualifications?

Instead of valuing differences, we often find bullying. How much is bullying costing us? How many of us have suffered the consequences of bullying? That constant:

> **"nit-picking, criticism of a trivial fault that is distorted, misrepresented, and added to with fabrication, those attempts to undermine you, being singled out and treated differently, being ignored, patronized, overloaded, humiliated, having your responsibility increased but your authority reduced, having leave (especially compassionate leave) refused, being denied training, having unrealistic goals set that change when it suits those in authority."** [19]

Some organizations are a hierarchy of unrealistic expectations and personal grievances pursued and enforced though inappropriate use of authority. There are layers upon layers of manifestations of bullying, from the chief executive who implies that his sales director should cancel his holiday because he 'wants a great result for shareholders', to the sales person who tells his prospect that he will 'be let down if they do not make the order'.

The impact of bullying is to decrease the individual's effectiveness by at least 50 per cent.

Some estimate that the impact of bullying is to decrease the individual's effectiveness by at least 50 per cent as the target copes with the physiological and psychological damage that is done. Therefore the annual cost to a business of each person who suffers serial bullying can be half their cost to the company, half the benefit that they were meant to bring, and reduce by a third the effectiveness of their colleagues. Of course the bully is often a complete loss – their ineffectiveness is only discovered when they leave.

Adding this all up and using research findings that indicate that at least one in every eight people is bullied then one estimate finds that the UK loses at least £32 billion every year (see www.sucessunlimited.co.uk/bully/typical.htm). That's around 10 per cent of public spending every year. How's that for shrinking the resources of a business or nation? Yet it doesn't feature on the political agenda.

Belief in the benefits of bullying others, especially where there is a grain of truth to justify the bully's actions, can be extended even to international affairs. George W. Bush's repeated statements that, 'Our nation, in our fight against terrorism, will uphold the doctrine of either you're with us or against us,' are open to misuse. The right thing must be done the right way otherwise, not surprisingly, it becomes the wrong thing.

Turning the other cheek is more than a nice idea. For many people of religious belief it is a requirement for spiritual development. Psychologically, it provides a healthy option to the shrinking feelings of resentment and bitterness. In the business world, it has been termed 'conciliation' and plays a major part in reducing the costs of disputes between employer and employee. Politically, initiatives such as the Truth and Reconciliation

Commission in South Africa have allowed the country to take tentative steps forward into a future free of blame. Symbolically, it is the only way towards a better world.

As Nelson Mandela put it: 'You can't make peace by talking to your friends. You have to make peace by talking to your enemies.'

If no one forgives, if no one is willing to absorb bad feeling and respond with goodwill, then a single fault can continue around the world, person to person, until **Life is not a Charles** everyone lives for payback and **Bronson movie.** revenge. Let's assign responsibility for actions, but let's allow justice to be sufficient and where justice is not possible then let it go. Life is not a Charles Bronson movie.

In the world of business, where some have tried to argue that the unforgiving, ruthless person has an advantage, the truth is that we avoid doing business with those who are likely to harm us if we make a mistake; we welcome relationships with those who are honest and understanding. Since we need relationships for commerce, the long-term advantage lies with those who are attractive to do business with.[20] Bullies can get a good press, puff themselves up, but they are invariably disastrous managers.[21]

But what do you do when you are really hurt by someone else? Surely, revenge is justifiable, even just? Isn't it reasonable to hate the perpetrator? Soon the hate spreads to not just an individual's actions but to everything about them, to everyone that resembles them, to everything that hurts you now or in the future. Hate *is* one of the wrongs that is done to us and it will keep hurting us for as long as we allow it to fester and dwell on it. Aren't there alternative approaches that will let you breathe, think and live again?

Consider the experience of Charlene Smith, a journalist who was violently raped by a stranger. She became a focus for the debate on rape and AIDS in her home nation of South Africa. She has become a national representative for what she chooses to call 'rape survivors'. Her story in the newspaper for which she works began, 'Every 26 seconds in South Africa a woman gets raped. It was my turn last Thursday night.' While she, 'does not want it to become the rest of her life', she has become an activist pressuring insurance companies, health care professionals, police, the government and counsellors to change their attitudes and actions. She believes herself to have 'been a catalyst', while 'there are so many people out there doing amazing things'. She goes on to say: 'I think people have been able to push more successfully for some of these initiatives because of the increased awareness of rape.'

Charlene Smith's actions after the rape were largely influenced by the way she was able to keep her 'mind strong and clear'. She explains that:

"There are times now and there will be times later when I will feel depressed and fearful. But he cannot imprison my mind. I have the power. He will never be as powerful as me. Even if he had killed me, he would have been left with the knowledge that I, and the others I am sure he has raped before, were the ones with the power." [22]

Charlene Smith has not allowed the rape to reduce her view of her own value. She believes that she has 'to turn this evil into good … Rape victims are not statistics, we are people, and this is our story. We have nothing to be ashamed of. It's a so-called moral society that does nothing that should be filled with shame.'[23]

Distorted perspective confuses us about what really matters and what really doesn't. The most troubling part of steroid abuse is the value that those who take them place on their potential benefits. Entertainers like Jesse Ventura, actors like Sylvester Stallone and body-builders like Arnold Schwarzenegger, have all taken steroids purely for how they make them look.

Those who start to take performance-enhancing drugs often start young and harbour completely unrealistic views of the advantages that those drugs give them. More than half of 200 recreational athletes said 'Yes' when they were asked whether they would be willing to 'take a magic substance that would transform them into uncontested world champions'. The athletes could live at world-record levels for a year, but at the end of that year, they would die. This is scary stuff when even the 'certainty of death isn't always a deterrent'.[24] The 'win at all costs' mentality distorts our perspective and poisons our relationships.

We can become similarly confused about work and life, forgetting which comes first! Sometimes we think that we are working for some purpose, making these sacrifices, working these long hours, but we have never quite linked the life we want to lead eventually with the life that we are living now. In the 1970s film 'The Wild Bunch', one of the hardened cowboys turns to another and states: 'I'd like to make one more score and then back off.'

His friend responds sceptically and piercingly with the question, '*Back off to what?*'

The strange thing that emerges is the seemingly elastic nature of resources when people are sufficiently well engaged. Tragedy often reveals the levels of effort and charitable giving that is possible. No one pretends that those that give go hungry or lose their homes as a result of giving, so why doesn't it happen more often?

We have never quite linked the life we want to lead eventually with the life that we are living now.

Any idea what you want? Perhaps you can see it exactly. Perhaps you can almost feel, taste, see and smell it. Maybe you are living the life you always wanted. It's just about possible that you still have no real, clear picture of what you want your life to be. It's also possible that you have not yet figured out how what you are doing relates to what you want.

MYTH WORK COMES FIRST

It is wise to take notes of the hero's words in the cult film, 'The Princess Bride'. He speaks to his true love, 'Life is pain! Anyone who says different is trying to sell you something.' Changing, unshrinking, improving, overcoming self-defeating behaviour, altering long-held but false prejudice and forgiving, all require real effort, even pain. This is not a popular idea. In our world, the only things worth pain are typically 'a six-pack stomach', a 'six-figure income' and the supposedly easy life that goes with it.

When enough people believe in the myth – that work is more important than anything else – then you find a conspiracy of compromise. Employer and employee both unhappy in stereotyped roles where they think that they have to remain.

It's the sad truth that:

"The workplace gives a lot of lip service to family-friendly policies, but when it comes to crunch time and a male employee isn't there, he's considered disloyal. In fact, if he puts his family first, he's considered a wimp." [25]

Needing money and the job that goes with it can lead to compromise after compromise until life becomes a tottering pile of them. Hey, we have all got to make decisions (finite time, finite resources) but let them be active choices. Figure out whether you really need to live the way you are living.

A friend of ours said to her husband: 'Just leave your job and do what you want to do – the worst thing that could happen is that you have to go back and get the same type of job again.' So figure out what the worst thing will be if you just do what you think will really be best. This isn't about self-delusion or obsession! It's about becoming a complete person.

We lead our lives with what we could term 'elective multiple personality disorder'. We can try to be a different person at work, at home, in our relationships, with our friends, in the quiet of our minds. This creates a lot of work! Not every personality is compatible – many say and do conflicting things. To be mentally healthy is not as easy as not being mentally 'ill' and what we are working towards here is mental fitness, health and vitality. Not the self-help, steroid-filled, aggressive mental muscles, but the peace that comes from knowing that you are one of the good guys.

What we are working towards here is mental fitness, health and vitality.

If you do too much of any one thing you will suffer the consequences of over-training. The natural balance (or homeostasis) of your body, mind (and soul) becomes disturbed, exhausted and will not return to normal without more than usual levels of rest. All people have their limits and when these limits are exceeded in any one area, damage can be done.

'Depression, fatigue, irritability, bad mood, anxiousness, confusion, excitement, desperation, lack of concentration, unwillingness to work, feeling of inability to go on, sleeping problems, bad appetite, shaking hands, abnormal sweating, palpitation, nausea, dizziness, obsession with work.'[26]

Which is more important to you – your life outside work *or* your work itself? Which is the priority? Where do you spend most of your time? Do you work to live or live to work?

When people are viewed as just another piece of office or business equipment, or even a job description or set of annual objectives linked to bonus schemes, they are reduced to simple, one-dimensional versions of themselves. Layers of humanity are stripped away or ignored so that only what is viewed as 'work related' is recognised or acknowledged. It can become so ingrained that workers themselves can believe that they should put their work before families, feelings and health.

Physical and mental health can both be put at risk by poorly designed jobs and sweat-obsessed working cultures. Many businesses still believe that more good is done in the long term if life and 'well-being' are sacrificed upon the altar of commitment. In this knowledge economy, we still have a majority who think that it is simply not possible to work too hard or give up too much for the business. Look at the following definition of work overload:

"Work overload is characterized by (usually a combination of) the following conditions at work: long and difficult working hours; unreasonable workloads; pressure to work unwanted overtime (paid and unpaid); [fewer] rest breaks, days off and holidays; faster, more pressured work pace; increased, excessive performance monitoring; unrealistic expectations of what can be achieved with the available time and resources; additional, often inappropriate, tasks imposed on top of 'core' workload (doing more than one job)" [27]

The Australian unions who produced that defining list of work overload estimate that each year it leads directly to stress-related costs of about 2 per cent of GDP (just as it does in the UK). In the USA, the total direct cost of occupational disease and injuries is more than $171 billion every year.[28] The unions that put forward these campaigns choose to focus on the argument that overwork is either just plain wrong for the employee (who should fight it on that basis) *or* that overwork costs more in injuries and disease than it brings in increased productivity. They take for granted the premise that workers exist to bring their bodies to work – the myth is unquestioned that life gets in the way of work.

AREN'T WE MISSING THE POINT? For the west there is no point competing with effort. The west cannot out-produce the rest of the world based on hours worked per employee. The cost of the labour gap is simply too huge to over-come by just staying longer at work. We have been overworking too long in the wrong areas. Economic growth is not fuelled by 'putting our backs into it' but instead relies on 'putting our minds into it'.

They take for granted the premise that workers exist to bring their bodies to work.

We need people who are capable of speaking up against the majority view, just as we need people who can support and stay loyal.[29] The two should exist for the same purpose: the better-ment of society and the world. Whistle blowing is a vital role that brings openness and scrutiny to illegal, ineffective, danger-ous and unjust situations.

In one such incident, Stephen Bolsin, professor and anaesthetist, went to the Press with evidence that cardiac surgery of children at Bristol Royal Infirmary was taking far too many hours to complete and had led to the unnecessary deaths of some of those children.

In another, yet more famous, case, Jeffrey S. Wigand used knowledge that he had acquired as an executive at a subsidiary of British American Tobacco to help win a $246 billion settlement to pay for the health costs of tobacco-related illnesses.

Why did they do it? This is Wigand's explanation:

"I am at peace with myself. I have a good name now. It's a very good name and I protect it very much. My name stands for integrity. I can't describe to you what it is like to have that feeling." [30]

PRINCIPLE 2 LIFE ALWAYS COMES FIRST

What do you want? Could a stranger know from observing the way you spend your time and energy what you really want and what you merely wish for?

Make it clear to your boss! Tell them that over the long term, nice people, nice companies, good people, good companies, do better, make more money and create more wealth than nasty, bad people and companies. It's a fact. The ethical indices created in the UK and the USA allow only those companies who meet certain ethical conditions to be included. Research studies demonstrate the same pattern, as we shall see in Chapter 3.

Companies included in ethical funds have strongly outperformed their rivals, yet they were not included because of their financial performance but because of their ethical performance. Over a five-year period these funds, including the Domini Social Index, within the S&P, and Goodmoney30, an ethical counterpart to the Dow, have beaten their competitors by several percentage points.[31] In the UK, the ethical FTSE4Good Index has outperformed the FTSE 100 and the FTSE All-Share Index.[32]

The nasty, the greedy and the dishonest will eventually fail. Just one example of this is Enron, which abandoned an ethical approach in pursuit of stock market popularity and short-term gains. It was an acknowledged polluter at home, an arrogant and careless user of assets in developing countries, and guilty of hiding the truth of its financial position from its investors. Now it is bankrupt and a former executive has committed suicide.[33]

A US Treasury spokesperson, commenting on the collapse of Enron said: 'Companies come and go. It's part of the genius of capitalism.' He was left asking: 'Are you sure that's a sign of genius? And if it is, why is that such a good thing?'

Why do we think that nice is more effective than nasty?

Why do we think that nice is more effective than nasty? You can probably think of more points, but try these for starters. Most money-making involves three groups of people – shareholders, customers and employees. It is more efficient to understand what customers want by figuring out their life styles than it is to just produce and hard sell.

That requires empathy and observation, both of which are easier for a person who is being genuinely nice. You can pretend to be nice but it is hard work! Similarly, employees need to be understood and they need to trust you if they are to follow you. Being nice, honest and generous is just easier to like and follow than the opposite. Only some kinds of dense shareholders prefer the hard-hearted company in the short term, because they think otherwise they are being weak. Maybe the unshrinking message will enlighten even the dark depths of their souls.

Reframe. It's an almost essential skill to change the presentation and meaning of what is said and done to you, and of the situations that you find yourself in – not to justify your own faults, but to improve your approach to reality.

When what appears to be reality leads to reactions on your part that are negative, the trick is to look again, redefining aspects of that reality until you see it in a more positive light. Once this is achieved, go back again and consider the original and the alternative views to see which fits the evidence best and is most helpful in dealing with the demands of the situation.

Some children do this naturally and we call it day dreaming. Teachers (and parents) tend to discourage one of the most useful and creative of our natural abilities. Victor Frankel used similar abilities to move his mind beyond the torture he experience in the Auschwitz concentration camp. He found we always have the freedom to 'choose one's attitude in any given set of circumstances'.

In a similar, although less serious, way, in the early 20th century, opera singer Florence Foster Jenkins belted out Mozart, Vivaldi, Bach and Brahms with great style and rhythm, but *stunningly out of tune* before elite East Coast audiences. Her career climaxed at Carnegie Hall. She reframed her pitch problems by saying: 'Some may say that I couldn't sing but no one can say that I didn't sing.'

You have to change your world with your mind and the efforts that follow. No one else can do that for you. You should expect opposition. Reframe and get to work.

Reframe and get to work.

Every day we may have to shift concepts at least seven to eight times per hour. In a typical workday, we could easily have to shift concepts 60 or 70 times! Each concept shift: responding to voicemail, email, internet, fax, pagers, cell phones, create stresses and perception problems in communication.

A 14-year study of more than 12,500 men in Sweden concluded that men with little control over their work were 1.83 times more likely to develop heart disease. Men who also had low levels of support in their work were 2.62 times more likely to develop heart disease.[34]

Depression has doubled with every generation since the 1920s. One million people per day in the USA are absent from work due to stress-related disorders. Some 72 per cent of US workers experience frequent stress-related physical or mental conditions that greatly increase health care costs. A landmark 20-year study conducted by the University of London concluded that unmanaged reactions to stress were a more dangerous risk factor for cancer and heart disease than either cigarette smoking or high cholesterol foods.[35]

As the neuroscientist, Karl Pribram, points out, noise in the system reduces the brain's information-processing capability.

The information age requires a new type of intelligence for people to sort through, filter and effectively process all this data. Stopping ourselves long enough to slow down and quieten down, so we can ask, 'What is really important? What would be the most energy-efficient way to handle all this?' can lead to intuitive answers that help us cut through complexity. To do this we need to find time to do it; but it quickly starts to save us time.

Oh yes, you can survive by thinking in nice, neat lines when life, problems and objectives are simple and fit into those nice, neat, lines. It's when things get messy that a different approach is needed. And tell me what you really think – are life's problems typically neat or are they messy?

It's when things get messy that a different approach is needed.

If you think life's problems are messy, and full of facts, then you will be better off using thinking that can cope with that complexity because it assumes that everything changes (it does), reality is contradictory (it is) and that everything is connected (what do you think?).

There are many ways of labelling this messy thinking for messy problems. Dialectical, inspired by Hegel, Socratic or Soft Systems Methodology, but (stay with us) we prefer to term it

Kirk Logic. We think it valuable because it seeks solutions where other approaches seek only to find the facts (Spock Logic) or problems (Bones Logic).

If you don't know 'Star Trek', think Aristotle, who preferred Kirk Logic to Spock Logic. Aristotle said the same; that rational, linear, provable theory is but one form of science. We also need judgement, wisdom and inspiration.[36]

Do we need truth telling and living by the truth? What happens in a world where we cannot even assume that others will keep their promises and give accurate accounts of events? How do we behave differently when others are likely to be self-serving liars, cheats and thieves?

If our society was less honest its progress and pace would slow. The evidence is there to see in each country that is less honest and reliable than the next. In some cases, corruption and unreliability plague governmental and commercial systems to the point where nothing can be planned for except bribes and delays.

Truth is an uncomfortable concept for some people because of its connection with lack of tolerance for ideas and actions of others. They fear that dominant groups will brand their own ideas as truth and the ideas of others as heresy. Our world has numerous large- and small-scale 'grand inquisition' equivalents and Torquemada act-a-likes. This may be cause for concern but it is only truth that can remedy such outrages.

It is valuable to learn what is real and seeking truth is part of that learning.

> "But also truth is an intrinsic value, that truth matters, truth is correlative with knowledge, I mean a falsehood is not an item of knowledge, and since knowledge is valuable and good to have, finding the truth about things is a good thing to do, so it is an intrinsic value in that sense." [37]

The 'truth' of something in isolation does not, of course, mean that it does not require care in its usage. Not everything that is thought or felt should be shared. Not every fact needs to be exposed.

There needs to be room to debate and think out loud without immediate (or any) condemnation. Without such debate, there is little scrutiny or discussion about what the real problems and solutions are. Instead, politicians (and the rest of us) feel forced to stay within the accepted boundaries of thought. What happens when the solutions are outside of those boundaries?

Why is such an artificial barrier put between work and life?

The Institute of Directors in the UK proudly announced, in 1999, that the European Parental Leave Directive, which offers parents three months' unpaid leave, would 'cost' business £35 million. But what about the cost to business of not letting employees attend to their responsibilities as parents?

Why is such an artificial barrier put between work and life? Why do senior executives compete for long hours, travel miles and stay nights away from their families? Why are phone calls or visits to and from family members during work hours viewed with such suspicion or even banned outright? Why are working hours left inflexible and closed to discussion?

Insisting that a person works so many hours that they never see their families cannot be good for longer-term economic growth. Tired parents do not read bedtime stories. Children who do not have this privilege fare less well academically[38] and emotionally.[39] How can that be good for the economy or individual businesses?

Working requires such a major part of our available time that we can start to believe the myths ourselves. Managers who make the rules often do so according to a significantly flawed value system that has been underlined and emphasized throughout high school, graduate, post-graduate and on-the-job training and education. They know something is missing but continue to chant the mantra that 'work is the only source of identity' and that all problems can be solved if only 'people would work harder'.

Convinced that they only got to 'where they are' by hard work and neglect of family and life, they insist that others do the same. Or at the very least they accept that it should be so or that it cannot be any other way. You don't have to force, cajole or monitor the work of those who love what they are doing. Listen to the enthusiasm two of those people who love their work:

"And every day, that's what drives me to get up in the morning and drive 80 miles an hour to work, and get here

as soon as I can, because I want to know what's going on. And it's not, 'Oh, I've gotta put in my time and punch the clock and get out of there'; it's 'I'm here to make a difference and I'm totally making an impact.' And that's what drives me. That's what makes it fun. It's – it's my life.**"** [40]

Once you have created work that people love the responsibility becomes to ensure that they stay fresh, that they do not over-train, become stale or burned out.

One of us once worked for a man who would insist that he did not pay for, 'my time', but that he paid for 'my ability to create ideas and make the right decisions'. So, he argued, I should stop the long hours, get out of the office, walk by the river, get an ice cream, hang out and listen to music. It took me a while to realize that the only link between the number of hours and the quality of my performance was one that was inverse.

This style of intervention is vital if the 'over-workers' (who think they are overachievers) are not to burn themselves *and* their colleagues out. The problem is that once even one person gets the work–life balance wrong it can start to tip the relative assessment of what 'a working day' means. Consider the following:

"It all starts with the overachiever. You know, that guy you always see at work, no matter what time of day or night you go in? People always talk about that person having no life outside of work, they joke and laugh about that person, but nobody seems to take it very seriously. That person is not

> only neglecting their own life, they are ruining things for everyone else that works there, and at the same time, ruining the entire culture.
>
> Eventually, you end up in a situation where if you aren't working at least 60 hours a week, you're passed up for promotion at the next review. And no one will come right out and admit that it's the reason. Or maybe you work the full 78 hour week and are still caught slacking some two hours. **"**[41]

The very ability to change and be flexible, that business leaders say they need, is reduced when people are over-worked and/or micro-managed. Over-work reduces creativity, rationality *and* the confidence to take risks. How many workers do we need who can't think straight? Do we think that our people will work more effectively when they are worried about home life? Do you believe that emotionally exhausted people will build better relationships with customers?

There is a reason that so many amazing entrepreneurs had their first breakthrough ideas while still at school or college – because they had time and room to think. Smart people will still make bad decisions and create sub-standard designs if they are too tired or stressed to think clearly. It takes even more space to be able to create effectively. How much 'room' is there in your business and in your life?

Here are some practical suggestions to unshrinking yourself:

Become one person

We need to stop wearing all of those hats, playing all those roles and thinking that one ability or strength compensates for not developing ourselves as complete people. Reduce the complication by being only one person all of the time until you become whole.

Get out

Get out of the house, get out of the office, grab a scooter, play with your family in the park, go see a band that you dislike, cheer the opposite team, imagine being your enemy, change political party, even if it's just for an hour. Then bring back some wisdom to your reality.

Adopt someone

Life is about relationships. In the end that is all there is. You don't have to adopt a child (although there are enough children who need parents) but you can attach yourself to someone else's welfare and help them win without any direct benefit to yourself.

Live your epitaph

How do you want to be remembered? What do you want your life to mean? Jack Welch wanted 'People Jack' to be his epitaph, but it will be the people around him who make that decision not him. What difference do you make?

We will need unshrunk people. We will need those who have a purpose beyond mechanically increasing production. That requires personal decisions leading to personal purpose. And purpose is a crucial turning point.

All life is sacrifice. All of life is choice. But sacrifice to what objective? Jack Welch, CEO of General Electric, sacrificed his life and relationships (what he called 'the biggest merger' in his personal life to do the 'the biggest deal' of his professional career –

In the end, you have to be your own expert.

but what did he gain? George Boutros, head of mergers at Credit Suisse, sacrifices a part of his humanity when he attempts to 'win and make you look stupid', in deal after billion dollar deal – but what does he gain? Three in four of all working people have sacrificed time with their children, their physical health, or their relationships – but for what?[42]

If we are going to sacrifice, then we should choose to gain something of enduring value. We will need a firm conviction of the benefits of a balanced life and the source of value creation if we are to plant now with confidence that we will reap later.

Lift others up? Create something of worth? Do the right thing under pressure? James Holub sacrificed his career in commercial land property to recruit youngsters, – 90 per cent of whom are drug addicts from Milwaukee's roughest areas – into a free web training programme leading on to careers earning an average of $63,000 after two years.

In the end, you have to be your own expert. An expert in you. An expert about you! An expert in what has an impact on you. Who should be more motivated than you to find out what drives you, how you think, what you need, and how to unshrink yourself? Who else is there?

Unshrink others

2

We are an inter-dependent species. We cannot do a thing without others. Just possibly you could survive alone on fruit on a tropical island, but it would not be pleasant, and even here your education and upbringing would influence how you could keep your wits about you. In every other situation we need others – teachers, farmers, suppliers, capitalists, workers, pupils, house-builders, refuse collectors, law-makers – but above all, teachers, because we rely on skills.

The ways to unshrink ourselves are rooted in unshrinking each other. We can overcome the superstitions that prevent us from developing our individual talents, but the fullest achievements are collective. The keys to open this door lie in a fuller and more rounded perspective of leadership and of teamwork than we are used to in the ugly stereotypes of politics and business.

The problem is that we have a limited view of leadership. The myths we discussed in the last chapter, about winning at all costs, come accompanied with a view of leadership as being reserved for a few, naturally gifted supermen and women. Or some people rush to the other extreme and say that we do not need leadership at all. This chapter will look at how we motivate and sustain each other; how acts of leadership can be small or great and are carried out by everyone. Let's look at the first great myth of this chapter:

MYTH THE BOSS IS SUPERHUMAN

In many ways, 'The boss is superhuman' is the most understandable of our myths. Supermen and superwomen do not necessarily have more ability than others, but in a few, rare cases they actually do, and combined with their natural charisma, the effect is indeed other-worldly. The most inspirational leaders in our lives are blessed with heavenly qualities. The hair on the back of one's neck

> **Charismatic leaders are not the only ones who can be divinely inspired.**

stands up on hearing Martin Luther King say, 'I have a dream', whether it is for the first or the 50th time. A charismatic leader takes one briefly outside of oneself and onto a higher spiritual plane. They can enable us to slip the chains of earth and live momentarily in the state of our dreams. It is a sublime, superhuman quality.

These glimpses can inspire us to build a better life. But they are momentary and such leaders are human. Moreover, charismatic leaders are not the only ones who can be divinely inspired – anyone can be and leadership is not the only skill. The meaning with which the phrase 'The boss is superhuman' is mythological emerges in the common assumptions that a leader does not have weaknesses, does not have vulnerabilities and does not need to continue learning along with everyone else. These are very damaging beliefs which limit us all, the leader included.

Good leaders recruit balanced teams; they give people confidence through accurate praise; they know their own strengths and weaknesses; they know when to delegate.

Where 'The boss is superhuman' is a truly damaging myth is where it becomes addiction to the notion of a ruthless, omniscient leader who eschews consultation and whose buccaneering sword can work miracles in our lives. The management writer Jeffrey Pfeffer has charted the dizzying obsession of investors and journalists with 'hero chief executives'. Those who were aggressively opposed to trade unions were particularly feted. Whether or not they were any good was immaterial. As Pfeffer himself devastatingly comments on Frank Lorenzo, scourge of the airline unions and erstwhile head of Continental Airlines, who received a standing ovation from students at Harvard Business School:

"This is the same Frank Lorenzo who, in the decade of the 1980s, took Continental Airlines into bankruptcy twice and led Eastern Airlines to its final demise on 18 January 1991. It is not just any business executive who can take the same company into bankruptcy twice, losing $2.5 billion in 1990, and completely ruin what was once the third largest airline in the industry, Eastern." [1]

The irony is that the desire among anti-communists for a capitalist hero like Frank Lorenzo leads them to worship someone who failed to deliver for them – in an identical manner to the adoring fans of communist leaders like Mao and Stalin.

In business, the desire for a buccaneering hero who can rescue shareholders remains strong. Consider the following extract from the *Financial Times*:

> **"Josef Ackermann [at Deutsche Bank] wants to strengthen the senior manager's role and turn it into something akin to a strong US-style chief executive. Executives say that he runs Deutsche's investment banking division with an 'iron fist ... The writing is on the wall for Germany's traditional Vorstand [management by collective responsibility].' 'The old consensus model is a hurdle to quick decision-making,' says Dieter Hein at Credit Lyonnais Securities. 'A strong CEO and clear lines of executive responsibility are a natural next step.'"**[2]

The plea of the executives referred to in this report is 'give me more power because I want it'. One would imagine that, given this enormous political pressure to rip out checks and balances on the influence of chief executives, there is a body of scientific knowledge demonstrating that an autocratic boss is better for shareholders, for staff and for society, than others. Those of us who hear the negative voice in our mind, 'Others know more than me,' can assume that the writer of this news piece is onto something that we are too dim to understand. But the truth is, he isn't. There isn't such a body of knowledge. Management thinker Henry Mintzberg has been charting what actually happens to hero chief executives and their companies. He finds an extraordinary rate of failure. Moreover those with MBAs, the highly prestigious badge of executive respectability, were no more likely to succeed than others.[3]

At this point, a reader may think: 'Ah but that doesn't mean that Germany has solved all the problems and that every company should be run by a committee.' This is true, but it misses the point: it focuses on structures, which are unimportant, rather than people, who are important. Of course it is better to have one good chief executive than five mediocre ones. But it is also better to have five good chief executives than one mediocre one. Leadership, teamwork and achievement are not the result of formulae or structural diagrams that can be drawn on pieces of paper. They result from mutual respect, allowing each other to grow. They are a function of people.

Leadership, teamwork and achievement are not the result of formulae or structural diagrams.

The burden of infallibility hangs heavily on the shoulders of the modern manager. They shrink themselves as well as others. They regard their employees as 'resources', and they regard themselves as being above the normal stresses and insecurities. They feel constrained to pretend they do not have weaknesses and do not need development and can work excessive hours.

Consider the following quote: *'If you are God, you are not trainable'*. This comes not from a 1930s dictator, nor from a Hollywood diva nor, as far as we are aware, from God. It was a favoured quip among a group of senior executives at an industrial group in northern Europe in recent years.

Chris Grant is a London-based consultant and executive coach who spends much time trying to convince people in senior roles that they need training and development as much as anyone. 'Male groups are the worst,' he comments. 'You get groups in male-dominated cultures where they believe that the boss is superhuman. One example is from a company forum where, when asked, not one person was prepared to say that they could have handled something better.'[4]

The result is stress, anxiety and fear of failure, long hours, health problems and poor decision-making.

There are situations where the leader does not know the task better than the experienced staff and is supervising a team of skilled people, carrying out complex tasks. The nominal leader could well be the least important person in the group and, in some cases, is probably not really needed. Sometimes groups of people collectively exercise leadership; not through any formal decision, but simply because all individuals know their task so well and know what needs doing that they simply do it, and naturally support each other while doing so. There are some highly skilled groups – probably more so in sports, families and clubs than in business – where non-verbal communication is both more instant and more profound than any formal instruction.

Recent research on learning shows that intuition, and an intimate knowledge of task and of context, are associated with the highest levels of mastery.[5]

When dealing with high levels of mastery, and a group where people know each other well, bad leadership is worse than having no formal leader. On other occasions, an individual unofficially takes the lead, where the named leader is absent or has not been appointed. This can be a source of relief for the other team members. The lesson is: *we can all show leadership to each other at different times, on different matters*. We can unshrink each other; take it in turns to be leader. The benefits are mutual and often multiple, and once you learn to do it, you can do it again. A receptionist can show the marketing director how to use Microsoft Power Point; a cleaner can advise a professor on how to handle relationships. It bears no relation to physical prowess. As the best school friend of one of us used to say: 'How is it that a five-foot, elderly female teacher commands complete attention, even from the roughest kids, when a six-foot, 30-year-old male teacher cannot?'

We can unshrink each other; take it in turns to be leader.

True leadership can be tremendously liberating, especially to people plagued with self-doubt, who need nurturing and inspiring. The leader does not bring everything, but they do bring something. It is not a gift given to a few at birth and hidden from the rest of us. This leads us to establishing the next great principle.

PRINCIPLE 3 WE ARE ALL HUMAN

Before giving some examples of great leadership, it is necessary to correct, or at least qualify, another, which is that: 'Successful leaders are strict – sometimes even terrifying.'

There is a tendency to simplify leadership types into polar opposites which are nurturing or dictatorial, nice or nasty. Successful leaders are neither or, more accurately, are both. They build people up and this gives a leader the credibility with which to direct and demand high standards. They do not skimp on praise. (Why are the rest of us so mean with praise, when we know how wonderful it is to hear? We comment on the way someone writes, answers the phone or corrects their child, and we seize on the error rather than comment on the strength.)

On pages 56–57 are some practical suggestions for consideration.

We help others and we help ourselves. That bit is easy. You could criticize us for being condescending, but what we are concerned about is the lack of action not the lack of belief. The need for philanthropy is greater than ever for the emotional development of the givers and the practical development of the receivers.[6]

And the sooner we give, the greater the impact of the gift.[7] We could call it 'compound giving' – which allows the giving to unshrink its potential for as many years and in as many ways as possible. We shouldn't feel guilty (or make others guilty[8]) about what we have but instead need to do something with it.

Give double

How often are you asked for help? How often are you asked for a charitable donation? Next time give more that you are asked for. In the USA, the average wealthy family gives 1.8 per cent of its income to charity but the average poorer family gives 4.3 per cent.[9] It will make you feel good all day, you will never miss it, and your money will unshrink. Instead of being spent on a new CD, dress or whatever, it will change a life.

Fight fear

It's strange how we don't do what we want to do and what has to be done because we are scared. We need to fight our fear and reach out to change the frightening situations that children and adults are in, throughout the world, as a result of war, torture, intimidation, lack of education and abuse.

Groundhog principle

In the Bill Murray comedy drama 'Groundhog Day', his character lives the same day over and over and over again. Each morning it begins again. At first he abuses the situation but then learns that a little preparation each day leaves him very prepared at the end of many days. He learns the piano, mouth-to-mouth resuscitation, patience, empathy and eventually finds true love. It's only a film, but what stops it working in our lives or the lives of those we can help?

Share in queue

Next time you are in queue in the supermarket or in the dentist's waiting room try talking to your neighbour about stuff that matters. It's amazing how many people sit in silence with problems, opinions and ideas that really need to be shared. Silence can be golden but it can also contribute to our shrunken societies.

Getting over the fear of helping other people, of saying what we think, of changing the world, is a necessary step to being a whole person. It's okay to be outraged with the injustices in the world. That's healthy as long as we do something about it.

Even the more coercive side of a good leader is really a form of love – they passionately want people to succeed. Only if the subjects feel utterly secure and entitled to express their abilities will the directive instructions have any positive impact. How about an example from the game of cricket, and a team captain who wasn't a good enough player? This team pitted ten against 11, in terms of playing ability, but they kept on winning, because of leadership. Here is what one player says about the captain. Note the qualities of respect, acceptance, empathy and awareness, but also the demanding of high standards. Asking for the last of these can only be done after establishing the former.

"There is no doubt that a large part of my early success with England was due to having Mike Brearley as captain ... [He] was different from the others. At a time when a lot of people had been treating me like an idiot, he went out of his way to deal with me as an adult. Most important, though, he *listened* to me. He knew that the success of any team is based on mutual respect. He also used to wind me up; he would say 'My aunt Fanny could bowl faster than that,' which would really get me going." [10]

The captain was a cerebral, gently mannered individual called Mike Brearley. Compare that with the bully Bob Knight from

Chapter 1. The player, Ian Botham, went on to become one of the all-time greats.

This approach to unshrinking yourself and others is just as effective in business as in sport. Sir Robin Saxby has led the chip design company ARM since 1991. It is now worth more than £3 billion. Like Mike Brearley he emphasizes something that is anathema to those locked in to 'The boss is superhuman' myth. This is the importance of listening to the newest or most junior member of the team. At its basic level, it is a form of hospitality, in the way that a healthy neighbourhood will give a voice to a new resident and seek to learn from the observations of the newcomer. In a company, this method encourages a good atmosphere and can help business. These and similar other skills are needed in leadership, as Sir Robin testifies. Again we see the common themes of listening, communication, learning, co-operation and ambition:

> **Even the more coercive side of a good leader is a form of love: they want people to succeed.**

"A bright young engineer, who might be a fresh graduate, could have a brilliant idea that ends up patented. This could be of more value to the company than exercises in saving. It is a case of recognising excellence. It is a lot to do with having people in the right jobs. The idea that there is a bad person or a good person is wrong; it is more to do with what they are doing.

'When we signed up with our partners, even in the early days, it was not just about 'Can we make money?' but 'Will

our partners help us achieve our objectives?' If our partners are not successful then we will fail. Both partners have to make money.

'People deal with people. In any company there are people of different types. You find people whom you can trust and can get along with; sometimes you look them in the eye and sometimes it is blind faith.

'If you do the right things by the customer you will succeed. Our culture is hard work and fun, but if you are not having fun you will not be the best.**"** [11]

True leadership expects high standards and is ambitious.

There is an extraordinary paradox here. The great leaders relinquish 'The boss is superhuman' myth – and end up being worshipped. True leadership expects high standards and is ambitious, but it depends also upon accurate listening, empathy and communication. This leads us on to the next great myth that needs tackling.

MYTH THE PLAN MUST BE SECRET

We depend upon one another for everything. But in our theories about work and economics, and in many assumptions about relationships, we pretend that we do not. This is most clearly exemplified in the secrecy with which senior management teams discuss their plans; or governments their intentions; or even academics in the language they adopt to share their knowledge. In the words of Eduardo Galeano, Uruguayan author and journalist:

"It taxes me even to read some of the more worthy books written by certain sociologists, historians or economists ... A closed language is not always the price one has to pay for profundity. It can hide, in some cases, an incapacity to communicate that is elevated to intellectual virtue. I suspect that boredom serves a purpose here: to bless the established order; to confirm that knowledge is a privilege of the elites." [12]

In most situations the benefits of a small cadre of people holding exclusively on to information are doubtful, to say the least. Does the employee of a call centre know what their main purpose is? Is it to serve the customer, or to answer so many calls per hour? How is a husband empowered by hiding from his wife the state of his finances? How can you empower yourself by hurting someone who is part of you?

This applies to business, politics, social groups and relationships. Experienced counsellors relate how individuals expect the people in their lives, most especially their partners, to *guess* what they want them to do in the home, the car and in bed. As beings we are extraordinarily gifted at communication, so what are the beliefs, the fears and the dogmas that prevent us from exercising this gift? Could it be a predisposition to treat others as enemies or potential enemies?

As media spread and become more invasive the natural reaction of some politicians is to become more defensive, or to try to trick the media through what is known in Westminster and Washington as 'spin'. There is an attraction to secrecy even where it does not serve their purpose. It is gradually dawning on politicians that such efforts are hopeless; it is almost impossible to disguise their fingerprints on any attempts to manage a news agenda and their

Lies only work temporarily.

efforts become a news item in themselves. Lies only work temporarily and even then they have to be woven in with a strand of the truth.

The tendency towards secrecy begs some fairly obvious questions:

- Who is the secret for?
- What is the purpose of keeping it?
- How will we be damaged by others having this knowledge?

But it demands a less obvious question also: How will we be damaged by others remaining ignorant of this knowledge? Is there any situation, other than the rare example of this other party being a mortal enemy, that withholding knowledge serves my interest?

In recent years, employers' organizations in Europe have fought a bitter campaign against consultative works councils in companies. They argue that they are being 'distracted' from running their businesses by being forced to consult with their employees instead; much as someone at relationship counselling might whinge that: 'Instead of being free to improve my marriage I'm being forced to talk to my spouse'.

Effective managers invert the onus. Instead of asking themselves 'Why tell?' managers consider 'Why withhold?' They do not pretend that their people are separate from their plans. Suddenly the whole body knows that it is about to start walking. Communication is wonderful. In its absence, every manner of fear, paranoia and suspicion creeps in.

This brings us to the sophisticated matter of language, and the degree to which cliques and inner groups repel outsiders. The creation of esoteric terminology is incredibly attractive to every profession, group or sometimes even couple, who wish to remain closed. In many cases, the effect is damaging for those within the group as well as for those outside.

The temptation among managers (along with many other professionals) to use a hermetic language, employing ever-changing jargon, creates a climate of secrecy and mistrust that corrodes trust. John Lloyd, a pioneer of the union partnership movement in the UK, describes how a young personnel manager was in a meeting with some seasoned trade union repre-

Most professions developed their own acronyms and jargon.

sentatives and talked to them about the need for a 'robust strategy, fit for purpose'. The union reps simply stared at her blankly. It was 'a failure, literally, to talk to one another,' he reports.

Those who use terms like 'win-win scenario', 'TQM', 'alignment of HR', 'fit-for-purpose' do not sound clever. Anyone who has worked on the shop floor has heard the sigh of weariness and cynicism that such phrases induce. There is a palpable drop in the energy and effort of everyone involved.

Managers are not alone. Most professions have developed their own acronyms and jargon. Where they are dealing with something technical, this is unavoidable; where they are dealing with people it is unforgivable. It can happen paradoxically when people are trying to overcome stigma; the unconscious desire to build a code defeats these efforts. Social workers, for example, in pursuing a more respectful language for people in their care, switched from the term 'mental handicap' to 'learning difficulty'. Unfortunately, at work, many social workers actually use the abbreviation 'PLD' (people with learning difficulties) as shorthand, and bandy the term about freely, which seems appallingly disrespectful. Most people would rather be called mentally handicapped than a 'PLD' – it sounds like a toxic chemical or a type of building joist. The people thus labelled are shrunk.

The desire to appear innovative causes many to seize the latest fad, wrapped up in its jargon. The impression that this forms in the minds of others is absolutely the opposite of that intended: they start to suspect that the professionals or managers using the terms are insubstantial and vague.

Take the following extract, from a paper on business process re-engineering:

"Evolutionary levels of transformation, that include local-ized exploitation and internal integration, leverage change enablers either intra-functionally or intra-organization-

ally, but do not question or significantly change the old course of action. Revolutionary levels of transformation, that include business process redesign, business network redesign and business scope redefinition, incorporate also questioning and changing the current operations. "[13]

Note the complete absence of references to people – they are shrunk to nothingness. When this happens, language is meaningless. The organization is taken to be some sort of inanimate machine or, at best, a single organic entity that 'evolves' (see Chapter 3 – Myth: organizations are machines).

Passages like the one above do not communicate, they intimidate – sometimes accidentally, sometimes by design. They reinforce the false internal voices that we hear that, 'Other people know more than me,' or 'I'm stupid.' They shrink us.

Withholding information is terribly attractive.

Sometimes, these sentences cause cynicism, not humility. How many senior managers have sat in a cubicle and felt the waves of despair and cynicism that overwhelm the staff when they hear a wave of management-speak? Conversely, have they felt the energy and dynamism that infuses the place when managers speak to the staff in a respectful, adult way and ask their opinion?

Withholding information is terribly attractive. It gives one power, but only relative to the person denied that power. Under the myths that inhabit political thought we are all supposed to be enemies with opposing interests, so it appears that damaging another constituency automatically enhances one's own. These beliefs have never been proven, and are quite wrong. The importance of recognizing inter-dependence in business and in society are explored in the next chapter.

Our employees, our customers, our suppliers, our neighbours, friends and lovers have a vested interest in our success, even if they do not realize it. If one does not recognize this, it is easy to fall into one of two extremes, to be a shrinking violet or a bully, neither of whom are terribly good at communication. If other people do have something to do with our success (success here is defined broadly, from launching a business, to helping a community, to bringing up a family) then it is better that they know that, that they know what you want and what you might do for them.

From the discourse above we can establish the following principle.

PRINCIPLE 4 ONLY THE GOAL UNIFIES

What else is there? When we go the same way we are unified. We can do that when we agree on the direction and set off together. So why are the managers so loath to share the goal, the plans and the secrets with the people who create the value and pay the consequences? Consider the following:

"On Monday morning we arrived at work and we were told formally that we were going to this hotel for an announcement on the future of the company. We were then called in and told that the company had been taken over. I guess the

deal must have been done, so they talked about what was happening. The guy looked quite shy. I imagine that it is a horrible job. He said 'Sorry; it is much worse than I had expected. In short, manpower is to be cut in half.'

Then several of the managers handed out sheets of green and yellow bits of paper, face down. The MD apologized, and said that he couldn't think of a better way of doing this ... If when you turned over the bits of paper you found your name on the green sheet please go to the back of the room, where a group of managers were there to usher you into a room and talk to you. If your name was on yellow paper you could stay in the main room and it meant that you were staying with the company.

One of the managers found he was going as well. I still remember his parting comment; he had been my manager – he was a lovely guy, quietly spoken – I said: 'Thanks, I have enjoyed working with you, you're a great guy.' He looked up and said: 'It doesn't count for anything, does it?'

I felt no sense of personal relief at all. We were given a spiel about the new company and how it was going to be a brave new future for us. Most of us were outraged because, to be quite honest, we just wanted to go with our mates. **"** [14]

The feeling of control that powerful people have by withholding information is often an illusion. In a real community like a company, a neighbourhood or in wider society, gossip increases in proportion to secrecy. If the people at the top, or in the inner clique, do not have a clue, that comes over more strongly, not less, if they say nothing.

These assumptions are even carried over in examples such as the one above, where the staff numbered several hundred well-educated people, mostly software developers. Now the managers at this company were not sinister, evil characters. They were nervous about making redundancies and had put some thought into lessening the blow. They would much prefer to have been announcing an expansion.

The myths are powerful but they are not inevitable.

But the habit of secrecy is strong and the examples of treating people as pawns are persuasive, especially in organizations. In the case above, the employees were expected not to use their minds, or engage their emotions. The managers considered it quite reasonable for those surviving the cull to be inspired by a talk on their future just a couple of hours after their friends and colleagues had been shown the door.

Negative myths persuade us to be cynical – that being good or doing good 'doesn't count for anything'. The myths are powerful but they are not inevitable. They are particularly rife in business, as we shall discuss in the next chapter.

Unshrink
your
business

"Organisation doesn't really accomplish anything, plans don't accomplish anything either. Theories of management don't much matter. Endeavours succeed or fail because of the people involved." Colin Powell, US Secretary of State

Unshrinking yourself, unshrinking each other, sound like great ideas. Looking within for development, and at friends and families for help, can be inspiring. But what if the immediate environment really does stink? At work the boss is a tyrant, the pay is low and there are few other opportunities. Time and money for further studies are difficult to find; there is a young family to feed. It would seem that the owners and managers of the big corporations gain tremendous profit from keeping people in this insecure, shrunken state. We will demonstrate that this is not so.

This chapter looks at business and trade union theories that pretend our interests never coincide, and we reveal their extraordinary similarity. It will show that we all gain when we allow others to grow.

Such thoughts do not provide immediate rescue for someone exploited, but they will provide a truer context. If one believes that one's misfortune is either inevitable or a price to pay for someone else's success, this can be terribly disabling. Overcoming such myths enables one to construct a rational case for a better deal, instead of just lashing out with the complaint, 'It's not fair!'

When the feeling grows that luck is the dominant determinant of success we should not be surprised when we see rioting in

Genoa or land grabbing in Zimbabwe. As long as these groups, of anti-globalists and civil war veterans respectively, do not believe that the G8 and farmers have earned what they have, they will protest. It doesn't matter, largely, whether they are right for now. The mere belief that something is unfair is bad enough.

The mere belief that something is unfair is bad enough.

Problems in business and management are caused by what is known as 'scientific management'. Although the term is not used often now, there have been radical departures only by a few brave souls, some of whose ideas become corrupted by the old myths.

The habits of 'scientific management' form the unspoken assumptions of most managers. The term arose from noting how the structure of a highly organized company could be likened to that of a machine, to which people are subservient as 'resources'; and that if one does this the people can be made to operate in the way they are ordered to, to maximize operational efficiency.

It uses concepts borrowed from engineering, so let us make a comparison with the real thing. Every engineer will assume certain things about background, constant factors. Without doing this, the calculations and formulae are too intricate and inconsistent to be usable. So the mechanical engineer assumes that gravitational acceleration is constant at 9.81 m/s^2 and the chemical engineer that there is perfectly even mixing of ingredients.

But what is the basic, operating assumption of the scientific manager? That people will not behave like people! It is an oxymoron, but most managers believe it. Everyone who defines flexible labour markets, operational efficiency, or 'synergy' from a merger, in ways that remove people and their motivations from the equation, is assuming that people will simply fall uncomplainingly into the new slot allotted them in the reconfigured machine. It is a theory that is not rooted in the real world. And in practice, it nearly always goes wrong.

This leads us to one of the key myths of groups and organizations, that is particularly rife in business.

MYTH PEOPLE OBEY ORDERS

The famous Hawthorne experiment in the 1920s and 1930s gave an early indication that the approach would lead to disasters. A perceptive researcher, the Australian Elton Mayo, carried out studies in an electrical factory in which groups of people were selected and the environment around them changed. For example, one group of workers enjoyed better lighting, while another select group suffered poorer lighting. In the first group, productivity went up. But in the second group it also improved.

Mayo concluded that the performance of the groups improved because they were paid some attention by managers and made to feel special. He realized that the emotional aspects of feeling valued by managers and bonding as a team were more important than the physical environment.

One oddity about the Hawthorne experiments has been their extraordinary fame in managerial circles combined with a complete failure to change attitudes and behaviours in light of the findings. It is an example of a common phenomenon, that sustains myths, where people observe evidence that their assumptions are baseless, only to respond by saying, 'Mmm, that's an interesting observation, now, moving on ...' and proceeding to behave as if nothing had changed.

The truly fascinating aspects of the celebrated experiment came in the details of the group dynamics that Mayo subsequently studied. He looked at one group of workers – comprising wiremen, solderers and inspectors – in great detail. Management writer Stuart Crainer takes up the story in his book *The Management Century*:

“The more the researchers looked at the group's behaviour, the more they uncovered. First, there were a variety of social structures at work. Being a wireman granted workers greater prestige – though not as much as being an inspector. This was revealed in the usual ways human beings find to express their superiority – soldermen were dispatched to get lunch for the group; wiremen exercised control over whether the windows were opened or closed. The good news for the soldermen was that there were people lower than them in status. These were the truckers who brought supplies and took away finished products. Truckers were put in their place by a variety of tricks and treats – including spitting on the completed terminals. All truckers were treated the same. New recruits were auto-matically treated in the same way as all other truckers. This was not written down in some corporate manual. It simply happened.

They conclude: 'The group created a complex world of their own. They exerted control over it.'**"**[1]

The pattern will be familiar to any manager who has started, fresh-faced and armed with the latest motivational and management theories, at an established company. They try to force change on the group and are puzzled when they find resistance, not only to ideas linked to the employees working harder, but also to initiatives designed to give them better salaries and more say.

People do not obey orders – and, in many cases, probably should not.

The dynamic is easier to understand when one recognizes that people do not obey orders – and, in many cases, probably should not.

International competition demands the kind of innovation and uniqueness that only the unique mix of people in an organization can bring. Difference. Difference. Difference. That allows best practise to work because it *is* customized to suit a particular circumstance. Difference is the friend of best practise *not* its enemy.

"There is always something uncertain, there is this wonderful phrase, 'Uncertain imitability,' which is actually the key to competitive advantage.

'The loss of freedom, discretion, autonomy is expensive, because in the end it doesn't work very well. Clearly defined, enforceable rules simply can't capture what makes a dynamic firm, an effective hospital or a brilliant school.**[2]**

Who is asking for all of these rules, measurements and league tables? Are they not simply being used *instead* of improving the way we do things? We need *workers that are more independent* and fewer managers. We need easier, simpler reporting mechanisms not more.

The history of our world teaches us that people are capable of remarkable achievements and that they are more likely to do them when they have principles and a lightweight structure around them to guide their actions. The extremes of anarchy and monarchy have not worked.

We need the *best* efforts of our people and that only comes when they are prepared and supported to improve and adapt to ever-changing circumstances *not* when we insist that they do exactly what they say.[3]

Very few management theorists have ever spent any time at a junior level in an organization. Even the more enlightened ones, who delve into motivational matters, will still tacitly assume that motivation comes from the managers and must be given to the staff.

Many managers see themselves, apparently, at the apex of the company, and assume that their insight, vision and worth are greater. It can be a tacit assumption, but nonetheless very strong.

There is a bigger idea, a stronger, older and more dangerous myth lurking behind all of this, of which the above discussion concerns largely its symptoms. This the implicit belief that when organizations become very large they are not really human communities at all. It is to this myth that we now turn.

MYTH ORGANIZATIONS ARE MACHINES

From time to time some top business executives gather in Lausanne, Switzerland, as guests of a training company backed by the toy company Lego. Executives are encouraged to make plastic models of their companies, break them up and rearrange them. It is called 'LEGO Serious Play'.

"The managers will be asked to use the blocks to build their own visions of the company they work for. Then they will be asked to demolish their model and start all over again. This is meant to be helpful in two ways. Holding a representation of their company in their hands is said to give managers a kick. And the speed with which these models can be built and destroyed is meant to teach them something about the importance of being adaptable." [4]

It is clever marketing by the Lego company and it bolsters the favourite instincts of executives. They love to restructure endlessly, searching for the optimum, 'efficient' structure. Thus they will outsource, then in-source; devolve to individual managers then centralize to control costs. During all these procedures the constituent parts of the company are called 'units' and the people therein 'headcount' as though a human enterprise was just building blocks.

Those who doubt the potency of the 'organization as machine' myth should look at the business pages of any newspaper on any day. The things that make the head-lines are the deals and the restruc-turings, as though the enterprises were inanimate entities that can be reshaped to suit the will of the senior executives. Then contrast this with the matters that actually

> **As though a human enterprise was just building blocks.**

drive performance. Rarely will a business editor lead on the story 'Bill Gates recruits entire graduating class from university', 'Bank trains all its staff in how to give exceptional service' or 'Retail enterprise discovers new market by recruiting ethnic minorities'.

One should also consider the very 'un-human' terms used to describe most management practices and fads. Business process re-engineering is the most obvious mechanical metaphor, but the general tendency to copy a practice from one to another, ascribe to it a new-fangled term, often reduced to an acronym employed as an unwieldy verb, indicates a tendency to assume that a large organization obeys some sort of mechanical logic. People have actually used the terms 'BPR' (business process re-engineering) and 'TQM (total quality management)' as verbs – so 'Have you TQM'd yet?' will be asked with a straight face.

At its most extreme, the separation of employees' welfare and development is so fiercely segregated from 'the company' that the attitude is even worse than taking a mechanical analogy. A 2001 report by the Confederation of British Industry, *Cutting Through the Red Tape*, uses conventional accounting to claim that measures on reduced working time and higher minimum pay 'cost' private sector organizations in the UK £12.3 billion. In an intriguing passage, however, the report grumpily mentions that the new rights 'have benefited some employees' as though a benefit to the employee has no benefit on the organization that the employee forms a part of.

This assumption is actually worse than taking a mechanical analogy. After all, it would be odd to claim: 'The servicing of this car came out at a net cost of $250. There was no improvement to the car, but there were some improvements to the spark plugs, oil quality and gaskets.' People are assumed not merely to be cogs in the wheel, but extremely unimportant cogs, whose maintenance is actually counter-productive to the smooth operating of the machine.

One would expect, given the dominance of treating organizations, particularly large ones, as though they were inanimate machines, that there is a bank of knowledge demonstrating that this method is effective – at the very least, for shareholders. There isn't. In fact, there is a surprising amount of evidence demonstrating exactly the opposite.

The most exhaustive recent survey was by the maverick business author Jim Collins. He compared the highest-performing companies (defined by return to shareholders) with 17 'comparison companies' which were not nearly as successful but which, in other respects, shared the same traits as the former group. The *systems, methods and approaches employed by the different firms* [our italics] were meticulously catalogued and compared. A write-up of the research in *Fortune* magazine concluded:

> **"Collins and his team searched for a correlation between executive compensation and performance, and found none. Ditto for a company's organizational structure."** [5]

The most revealing aspect of the research Jim Collins has undertaken is not the results but the questions. Why were such illogical questions asked? It is the equivalent of asking whether red cars are faster than yellow cars. If we began with the starting assumptions that organizations comprise people, that language is imprecise and that people are complex, we would never spend so much time exploring whether these mechanical metaphors were accurate or not. We would have known that they were not. Still, it is useful to have such conclusive evidence.

> **But most managers *believe* that they are succeeding.**

Collins' research does not have to stand on its own. The *typical* failure rate of the contemporary executive intervention based on the 'organization is a machine' myth is 70 per cent. Some 70 per cent of mergers fail; 70 per cent of outsourcing projects fail; 70 per cent of business process re-engineering projects fail. They fail at this rate by their designers' own measures – profitability and return to shareholders. We list some of them in the rest of this chapter.

But most managers *believe* that they are succeeding. In one study, 83 per cent of mergers were found to have failed to boost shareholder value, but the same proportion of managers believed they had been successful.[6]

One enters the supremely confident world of management expecting to encounter established modus operandi built upon accumulated knowledge that approximates to a rational theory. It's a world that believes the following myth.

MYTH ALL CHANGE IS GOOD

Management is a strange world where woolly notions like 'synergy' or 'efficiency' are venerated, but tangible principles like trust and caring are regarded as soft. The real becomes virtual and the virtual, real. Where shaking things up is expected to improve performance rather than simply lead to dizzy people.

Of course, evidence is never strictly objective or conclusive, but at least for the principles there is evidence. For the myths, there is none.

Business obsession with the bottom line is damaging. Corporate belief that being efficient is an answer in itself is wrong-headed. They both lead to a strange devotion to strategies that do not work. Period.

Business loves mergers – to the tune of some £2 trillion annually – because mergers promise efficiency. If you get rid of enough people but keep the same customers the result, the merger cult chants, will be greater profits. So why doesn't anyone mention that 70 out of every 100 mergers fail to add value? Why don't they acknowledge the fairly obvious point that customers can shop where they choose?

Study after study has shown that economies of scale from mergers will not automatically increase profits even if they reduce costs. And in the medium term, say 12 months, they don't even increase the share price. It's easy to reduce costs. Try it. Stop spending. See if you make any more money and have any more customers at the end of the month. Dare to try it?

Elsewhere, or sometimes in the very same merger-crazy companies, business process re-engineering (BPR) continues to do the rounds. It's popular because it promises higher profits. It is believed because it preaches that people are less important than processes in the pursuit of profit. So why doesn't anyone mention that, according to its creators, around 70 per cent of BPR projects fail?[7]

If people are treated like interchangeable 'resources' why should we be surprised when they all 'act the same'? Why do we assume that because someone resists change that they are wrong and that the change is right? There is a strong link here with the myths from Chapters 1 and 2. If people are assumed to be 'resources' slotting into a machine then it follows that the damage caused by a bully will be overlooked and the benefits from unshrinking an individual or team will be ignored.

PRINCIPLE ONLY GOOD CHANGE IS GOOD

The people who do the work are the experts. If they are not then start by helping them become experts before you rip up their work, take away their control and remove forever their commitment to it.

James Champy, the architect of business process re-engineering, has since acknowledged that people and teamwork are impor-tant. But he hasn't yet written a book to apologise. Which is a shame because there are still CEOs out there who think he was right.

Why didn't Nasser just come in and ask how he could help everyone achieve more of the same?

Consider, if you will, Jacques Nasser. When he took over as CEO of Ford Motor Company in 1999, the company had $10 billion in cash sitting in the bank. They had enjoyed a record year. So why didn't Nasser just come in and ask how he could help everyone achieve more of the same?

Instead, in pursuit of superstardom, he started to mess around with a culture that *was* performing: from his billion-dollar acqui-sitions of other companies, to his visible pleasure from his fleet of company jets, to the way he took a cynical chainsaw to union relationships and managerial pay in open homage to General Electric's Jack Welch. The joke at Ford was:

"Welch is surrounded by ten guys who will take a bullet for him, while Nasser is surrounded by ten guys who want to put a bullet in him." [8]

Result? Low morale (people hate it when you try and cheat them), law suits (on grounds of racism, sexism and ageism); quality levels (once the best in the industry) are worse that all main competitors; the car models are old (they only sell with interest free loans); the company is divided and confused; and Jacques Nasser becomes the ex-CEO of a company losing $1 billion a year.

Why this obsession with imposing just the right structure when extensive research shows no correlation between it and performance?[9] Don't they research before they decide? Why do they think that all change is good?

Why do they focus on deals, strategy, accountancy and marketing rather than career development, training and welfare? Maybe because these so-called 'hard issues' are easier to think about when your ego is too inflated to make room for other people.

Even the self-obsessed would prosper more if they avoided the urge for drastic and sudden reorganizations. Long-term research makes it clear that people cannot improve when they are busy coping with abrupt, unwelcome changes. We need to know that we have a future with an organization, that our welfare and development is central, before we will give it our best efforts.[10]

Is it such a surprise that financial results improve when people are committed? Differences between the ways people are treated have been found to explain 19 per cent of the variation in profitability.[11] Naturally, the same study showed that differences in investment into research only accounted for 6 per cent while technology registered just 1 per cent.

If you think from an unshrink perspective, it is blindingly obvious that firms that make development of their people a fully strategic goal will perform spectacularly better than others, as research at Rutgers University found.[12]

The international consultancy Watson Wyatt's human capital index makes it clear that adopting the best practises to employing people can add up to 30 per cent in shareholder returns over a five-year period.[13] All you have to do to experience those gains is have a collegial, flexible workplace, clear pay awards, honest communication, and management accountability to those they manage.[14] Research from the Hay Group shows that the people skills of a leader contribute up to 70 per cent of the factors that determine organizational climate and that this climate in turn can add 25 per cent to business returns.

The people skills of a leader contribute up to 70 per cent of the factors that determine organizational climate.

The Gallup organization compared scores for employee engagement and profitability, sales, employee retention and customer satisfaction for 7,939 business units, teams or workgroups in 36 companies. It found that 'The correlation was positive: highly engaged individuals were most often found in the high-performance units.'[15]

What else did you expect? How much more proof do you need? We know that the research we have quoted from will have the odd flaw or inaccuracy. We recognise that it is not 'pure' science but taken together it represents a decade's worth of empirical evidence from experienced researchers, all asking more or less the same question, and all coming up with the same answer:

> The way we manage people is the way we manage. If we un-shrink the people the organization succeeds.

If you put these findings in an easy-to-read format to a conventional manager or investment analyst, some will respond by saying, as we have seen before, 'Mmm, that's an interesting observation,' before changing the subject or muse that, 'This won't happen in our takeover of Stubborn People plc because we have cost savings, synergies and consultants on our side.'

They avoid the need to change themselves and they continue to force unhealthy change on others. They must think that they are helping themselves or why else would they do what has been proven to fail?

In the light of the overwhelming evidence that downsizing and business process re-engineering led to some ghastly mistakes, even some of its architects have acknowledged that they 'forgot the people element'. This apology is a bit feeble. No one would cheer zoologists who announced that, after 20 years of study, they had recognized that the effort of termites was, after all, an important part of the process of making termite mounds.

Why is the recognition so muted? Because the myths are so firmly embedded that management thinkers, even the better ones, often try to insert people, or emotional intelligence, into the machine, instead of scrapping the machine.

The consultancy KPMG publicized the fact that 83 per cent of mergers fail (see earlier), but can only timidly recommend that 'soft keys' – the people issues – should at least be of equal importance to the 'hard' matters.[16] This seems inadequate.

Insist that there is something fundamentally wrong with an approach that nearly always fails.

After all, if it transpired that, say, 83 per cent of surgical interventions using a new technique failed – that the patients would have lived longer without going under the knife – would it be enough for the doctors to say, 'Well, that's interesting; maybe we should tinker with the way we do the operation; adjust the balance a little'? A better reaction is to insist that there is something fundamentally wrong with an approach that nearly always fails.

We see the rediscovery of people as a fad to be appended to the mechanical metaphor. There are new-sounding theories known as 'Customer Relationship Management' or CRM. Another is 'human resources strategy in line with the business' or 'strategic HRM'.

In these newer approaches, people have been promoted! They are still cogs in the machinery but now they are more important, more sophisticated cogs. It is not enough. And it won't unshrink us.

Above all else, we need a more human vocabulary to describe organizations. Words like morale, customer delight, common purpose, fear and hope are more accurate ways of describing organizational life than 'CRM processes' or 'strategic HRM'.

The Gallup organization finds itself similarly limited by mechanistic views of an organization. Its study of more than 7,000 business units clearly shows that employee engagement leads to high performance and yet it concludes that:

"Employee engagement is far from the only driver of desirable business outcomes. Management tactics, procedures and human invention also contribute to improved revenues, customer loyalty, higher productivity and so forth." [17]

What else are 'management tactics, procedures and human invention', if not the result of employees' efforts? Managers and inventors are employees, too! Employee engagement is everything. It *is* management.

A more encouraging development is that of intellectual capital. At least here there is an attempt to put human skills and future potential on the correct side of the balance sheet – as assets – and therefore on to the agenda of managers. There will always be room for error in such measures, but it is an intelligent attempt to address the chronic weakness of looking only at historical transactions based on costs and fixed assets.[18] The point to make here is that it is not only intellectuals who matter, and that adopting the measures without ditching the failed metaphor of the machine will be insufficient.

The mechanical model is so pernicious it actually causes people to try to persuade good managers to abandon good practice. Take the recent quote from Gary Kelly, the Chief Financial Officer of the hugely successful Southwest Airlines in the USA.

> **"**I do get asked on occasion by investors 'Could you cut your costs in this area [recruitment and training]?' But if you are not going to work hard to get people who are a good fit, it will hurt you. For example, we have never had a strike. What airline is even close to being able to say that?**"** [19]

Investors and commentators are pleased with the way Southwest Airlines operates; but they are in stubborn denial of the factors that cause it to be successful – to the extent of trying to persuade it out of its good habits.

Why is this implicit belief in the machine so strong?

Praise for the airline tends to highlight features that can be described as being close to the mechanical norm of the most efficient company. Its fast turn-around times are praised as efficient and its strategy of finding a niche is celebrated. But this is to focus on effects, not causes. Southwest Airlines does not succeed because it has an efficient process for turning round an aircraft and starting a new flight; it succeeds because its well-trained, carefully selected people want to serve the customer and cause them minimum inconvenience.

Why is this implicit belief in the machine so strong? It goes back a long way. Look at the observation by British economist John Maynard Keynes:

"Practical men, who consider themselves above any intellectual influence, can usually be found to be the slave of some defunct economist." [20]

Some would say Keynes is now a 'defunct economist'. We agree with him on this point however. Nearly all managers believe in the theories of Adam Smith; and nearly all trade unionists believe in the theories of Karl Marx. The problems with the theories are the following: they are very similar, and they are completely wrong. Summarized, they are:

- For every economic gain there is a corresponding loss.
- 'Labour' behaves like a single entity.
- Economies are systems.
- Interests of different constituencies are automatically opposed.

It is difficult to root out these myths, because they are so much part of our everyday assumptions.

An example: it is common for redundant workers or trade unionists, when hearing of a lay-off plan, to complain that: 'It's profits first, not people.' The research we quote above indicates that only some cases of redundancies help the business succeed, and that in all cases the managers making the plan have absolutely no idea whether it will help the business or not. They are guessing.

So when the workers or trade unionists say that, 'It's profits first' they are giving the executives plaudits that they do not deserve. They also want to pretend that managers are succeeding. The roots of this lie in the theories of Karl Marx, as we shall discuss below.

In management, Adam Smith's ideas led to scientific management, sometimes known as Fordism or Taylorism after Henry Ford, who introduced the moving assembly line for cars, and Frederick Taylor, who introduced time and motion studies. Both these highly influential thinkers employed a systematic approach to the organization of work, in which the tasks were meticulously studied and broken down into components, with a limited number of tasks given to each worker. It was not all bad. Some of the improvements designed to save time will certainly have improved the ergonomics for the operators, as Ford sought to minimize any bending or stooping that they had to do. He also doubled wages to reduce staff turnover.

But he still looked at the system, not the individuals. While there were productivity gains in the early years, the extreme forms of Taylorism broke down in the anarchy and protests of the 1960s and 1970s, much of which was centred on the car industry (in the west only as Japanese car companies had dealt with confrontations earlier).

Moreover, scope for discovering the sort of massive productivity gains that derived from development of the moving production line is getting less and less. As the figures constantly show (but to which most managers pay only cursory lip-service), fixed capital and technology is shrinking rapidly as a proportion of a company's assets.

Both Taylor and Ford were really just building on what had gone before. Many Victorian economists and thinkers seemed to take the then new industrial machines as a metaphor for organizations.

Thus in the mid-1800s we find Karl Marx writing: 'In handicrafts, the workman makes use of a tool. In the factory, the machine makes use of him.'[21] Wrong! It is a *person* forcing other *people* to work at the pace of the machine. It *is* exploitation; but done by people, not machines. Marx goes on to refer to the factory as 'a lifeless mechanism independent of the

> **The truth is that factories are made, designed and run by people.**

workman'. Here is a myth at its genesis. The truth is that factories are made, designed and run by people. Exploitation is the result of bullying – a dysfunctional relationship. It is simply passing the buck to blame some lifeless machine called capitalism.

This remains a topical issue. Left-wing thinkers and trade unions describe capitalism as an inanimate 'system'. It stems partly from something called Karl Marx's theory of surplus value. This is one of the most powerful and widely held beliefs in the world of work. Very few trade unionists do not believe it. Every left-of-centre politician, however moderate, who denounces profit making, fat cats and the private sector believes in it, deep down.

It goes something like this. If you work for $10 an hour, making goods that sell for $100, and other costs come to $20, then for the first six minutes of every hour you are working for yourself.

For the next 12 minutes you are working to cover the incidental costs of producing the goods and for the next 42 minutes you are lining the pockets of the shareholder. The mere act of making a profit is by its nature exploitative.

The Alan Parker film 'Come See the Paradise', set in California in the Great Depression, gives a dramatic illustration of the theory. Jack is a dedicated workers' activist. His brother Gerry a factory worker with a family. Listen into their heated debate:

Jack: All I'm saying is, if you are getting one dollar fifty an hour and some guy in a suit is getting ten dollars out of it then it ain't fair – it's got nothing to do with Communism.

Gerry: It's got everything to do with it! I tell you: I'm glad I work there.

Jack: You don't know what you're talking about

Gerry: We should all be lucky to have work! Every time I go through those gates, I look up at the big sign and I say, 'God bless you' because some poor sucker ... is out there begging for a cup of coffee.

Surplus value possesses an attractive simplicity to Jack and many like him. The trouble is that it excludes some of the most important issues.

To begin with, it ignores the passage of time. This matters in a number of ways. First, the future value of the learning that the worker may be gaining in their hour of working can be considerable and this might more than outweigh the apparent losses by working for most of the hour for someone else. The surplus value calculation takes the worker and boss as being curiously isolated from the rest of the world. There is no notion of interdependence; that the proprietor gives as well as takes; that they are a worker too.

Secondly, where is the customer in all of this? Is the product or service worthwhile? Holding down a job while holding a Marxist philosophy is terribly dispiriting. You are telling yourself, and your comrades are telling you, that 'all' you are doing is lining the pockets of a rich person who does not need it; that your efforts are utterly worthless. Is this true of the engineer who makes stair-lifts and wheelchairs for a profit-making company? Is it true of the Nokia salesman who promotes the WAP phone that the anti-globalization campaigners use to arrange their protests? As with the capitalist, classical economic theory, the customer, the relationships and the inter-dependence that make economies work simply do not appear.

Would you rather earn 1 per cent of Microsoft's profits or 95 per cent of the corner shop's profits?

Thirdly, the proportion that a worker may be earning fluctuates with time. The Marxist critique is that the management will always seek to reduce the proportion of the hour that workers are working for themselves. Now of course many managers give Marx some ammunition here, and do indeed try to do so, but they are not behaving in a scientific way by doing so, and they are not boosting profits.

Another, even more basic problem with the theory is that it only discusses ratios, not absolute amounts. Would you rather earn 1 per cent of Microsoft's profits or 95 per cent of the corner shop's profits? Or have a share in a co-operative that is struggling to break even and may have to make you redundant next week?

Turning to Adam Smith, we find not the opposite, but the same argument. He says that 'labour', i.e. the mass constituency that forms the working population, behaves like a commodity. If it is too expensive, it has to reduce itself in price to make itself attractive to employers. Every gain for 'labour' means a loss for capital. Again the skills, morale, teamwork, relationships, people, shrink and disappear. It is lunacy turned into theory turned into myth,

---

Here's a summary:

What Karl Marx says
Profits come from reducing the hourly pay rates for the worker.

What Adam Smith says
Workers lumped together represent 'labour', the only important thing of which is cost, and profits come from reducing costs.

What actually happens
Profits come from customers buying stuff. Whether they want to buy depends exclusively on employees, the cost of whom is relatively unimportant.

---

but accepted as fact, leading to the Confederation of British Industry, in 2001, claiming that better conditions for workers 'cost' £12.3 billion per year to business.

You may well ask: if these theories of Smith and Marx are so wrong, why are they so popular? Good point. But we are only dissecting the economic theories here. Look at the philosophical themes these two thinkers addressed: Adam Smith called for freedom; Karl Marx for justice. These are two precious babies to keep hold of as we throw away some mucky bathwater. (Notice also how the myths pit these values against one another.)

The other point about exploitation being a form of bullying, not an arithmetical formula, is that it explains why it goes on in charities, trade unions and pressure groups, some of which exploit staff and volunteers, taking too much advantage of their willingness to help the cause. Many who have been involved in such organizations cheerfully discuss, in private after a long, poorly paid day, how ironic it is that it is actually nicer to be working for MacDonald's or Cisco, where you have career progression and better pay.

Are we are trying to unshrink the world with shrunken people?

This is a big deal! If employee organizations and pressure groups treat their own staff worse than multi-nationals then we need to think hard. Are we trying to change a machine with a machine? Are we are trying to unshrink the world with shrunken people?

Are we assuming that good intentions are better than good results? What does the anti-capitalist want to replace the hated machine with?

Organizations, political movements and economies comprise people. The way we treat each other can never be reduced to the status of being a means to an end; how we treat each other is the only thing that matters.

Communist organizations comprise living, breathing human beings rather than faceless agents in the class struggle. This has its good side. One of the most impressive organizations in the world is the Cuban health service. Its people can offer preventative and curative care on a par with a western European state. Its heart surgeons are world class; its deserved reputation is such that people visit for treatment not only from neighbouring Latin American countries, but even western Europe and North America. People can receive the best treatment at a fraction of the normal cost.

Researchers work closely with hospitals and some clinics have pioneered genuinely new treatments, especially in the area of dermatology and eye treatment. Researchers work in their own clinics and have considerable freedom to explore new techniques.[22]

Figures from the World Health Organization show that the Cuban population has mortality and morbidity patterns similar to those of a developed country. For such a poor country to have achieved this was one of the most impressive achievements of human endeavour of the 20th century.

One detail about the service embarrasses the capitalist and the communist simultaneously: it is one of Cuba's biggest export earners. It is a successful business. It employs cutting-edge technology, and displays all the features of the classic business clusters like the Japanese motor industry or Silicon Valley, with close cooperation between research establishments, the state and the enterprises. A researcher from the R&D department of a pharmaceutical multinational company would feel perfectly at home in the Cuban laboratories that developed new treatments for vitiligo and psoriasis.

The Cuban health service is one organization that understands that our next unshrink principle.

PRINCIPLE 6 THE ORGANIZATION IS A COMMUNITY

What else could it be? And if it's a community then you will want to concentrate efforts on building relationships. You will want to reward community spirit. You will want to ensure that everyone is involved.

Consider the Swiss-UK medical company, the Generics Group, that monitors the contribution that every person makes to the group and *not* only its scientists and consultants. Administrators and secretaries are offered above-average salaries and the chance to own shares. Consultants are rewarded for teamwork just as much as technical achievements or patents filed.

Jon Sparkes, Head of Personnel, says that many employers are misled by the conventional accounts and the focus on costs.

"The argument for cutting jobs or pay as the first thing to do when there is a downturn is that in companies like ours salaries are the most expensive item. Well over half of expenditure is in salaries. But when you implement a pay freeze you are not reducing those costs much; only that bit of the profit and loss that is the annual increase. It is the wrong thing to cut even financially.**"** [23]

Moreover, if cutting staff or salaries is the first option, then people are upset and someone you do not wish to leave may well go. You may be able to do away with your janitor, who has served you faithfully for 15 years. You may not care if he is upset at being summarily dismissed to save costs while a machine takes his place. But he could be the best friend of your star programmer. They go to the football together; they were best man at each other's weddings. Your janitor gets a job with your competitor – and so does your best software developer.

'Our highest fee-earning people are bringing in four to five times their salary. It is a bad move to do something to that person to make them leave,' says Sparkes.

So, try out the practical unshrinking suggestions on pages 102–3.

Here is another exercise for managers:

Next time you want to say 'the department' or 'the division' or 'the unit' say 'the people in the department/division/ unit'. Use this construction every time.

If you don't like our priorities then make up your own for responding to people as they really are. If business is a community and value is only created by the unshrinking principles, what difference does that make to the way that your organization is run?

Take as an example, Brad Hill, an unconventional pay consultant for the global personnel consultancy Hay at the group's office in Chicago, USA. He gave up advising wealthy executives and began helping hourly paid staff improve their working lives and their income. In his words:

> **"When I look at an organization, the people at the top are self-motivated; they are being taken care of. In the USA, we have done a dreadful job at bringing dignity and self-esteem to those who can make the biggest difference to productivity and to the customer; the people most important for delivering the work product or service.**
>
> **Unshrinking the people is really about bringing dignity and self-respect in all work. Much of my motivation comes from my grandfather, a coal-miner, who worked like hell his entire life and did the best he could. His company took his dignity and self-esteem away from him. It made a big, burly coal-miner a very fragile individual who had a nervous breakdown and who would be depressed because he "would never be anything but a goddamn coal-miner". My role is to bring dignity to miners and meat-packers and hospital workers and show them that their contribution is valued."** [24]

Management trust systems

Trust is more valuable than control in any organization, so establish ways of increasing the level of trust. In this way secrets will be shared, rules will be abandoned, work will start to have meaning and customers will keep coming back. Find out why trust is limited and then work until it is restored. Don't fool yourself that things will be good without trust. They won't be.

Reverse hierarchy

Which end of the organization is most important? The top or the bottom? Which one can your organization live without? Get the people at the bottom involved in strategy formulation and decisions! Get the people at the top down to where the work gets done with the real work experts. Not a one-off publicity exercise but a permanent feature of the way that you organize work (look at Robin Saxby in Chapter 2).

Honesty bulletin boards

Anonymity brings honesty. People say what they would not say without it. Any organization needs to know how people really feel and every person needs to feel that they can say whatever they want. Establish an anonymous internet bulletin board, keep reading it and do something positive about even (what you feel) is unfair criticism. At the very least respond (anonymously!).

Unshrink action and strategy

To unshrink people will not happen by accident. It's going to require a lot of desire and action. Everyone should have objectives (including the organization) for becoming more COMPLETE. The organization should do good deeds, support family life and relationships, view parents sports days as a priority, offer any level of training to any person, discover people's dreams and their problems and ensure that work helps with both.

What Brad Hill does is devise pay schemes where a team of ordinary employees decide, within certain parameters, which bonuses they will receive for certain improvements, be it in a cheaper process or a better product or service. These are known as 'gain-sharing' plans. His teams are randomly chosen, there are no 'employer's pets or union's pets', he pledges, and the schemes are long-term, designed to produce lasting benefits for all parties over several years. He finds such strong scepticism and wariness among staff that for more than half to be fully committed to such plans after a couple of years' work represents high achievement. Where this does occur, the mutual benefits are enormous.

One skill that Brad Hill teaches all the groups he works with is juggling. It is not compulsory, but there are lessons in the lunch break. It helps people learn that learning can be done and can make you feel better about yourself.

"Every single participant thought that it would never be possible. You have preconceived notions. You throw the balls to the middle, not in a circle. It is a question of overcoming perceptions of how you think something is done. You have to listen. You have to fail about 500 times before you start to get it." [25]

If you are not lucky enough to work at a plant with a pay scheme designed by Brad Hill, you can still teach yourself juggling, learn a new technical skill and go for that promotion.

Contrary to another unspoken managerial myth, people do not become more stupid as one goes down the hierarchy. The receptionist, the cleaner, the post-room manager and their dog knows when the top management does not have a clue. Departure from comprehensible language is the surest sign of this malaise.

Don't believe so slavishly (and complacently) that the reward system does what it purports to do. It is still implemented by people who give favours and have favourites. The 'system' must be replaced by self-determination within limits that are agreed and changeable by the person who is living within

> **You can still teach yourself juggling, learn a new technical skill and go for that promotion.**

them. Let that person decide what they want and then figure out what they are willing to do to get it!

Our academics have dreamt up, and then experimented with, ways to modify the behaviour of rats and of people who do jobs that require rat-like levels of intelligence.

Behaviour Modification[26] or B Mod, as it is affectionately known in management circles, stops being effective, according to one MBA text book, when 'tasks become more complex and require more creativity'[27] but it still goes on to explain its virtues. WAIT A COTTON PICKING MOMENT! Is not the challenge of advanced economies to finds ways to create ever-more creative, intelligence-packed products, and interlinked, multi-level experiences? Isn't the world of work becoming, at all levels, more complex? So why worry about motivational systems that have struggled to motivate even in jobs that demand so little of their workers?

Why waste your time trying to make the dull interesting when you could simply give your teams interesting jobs in the first place? We need culture modification that will lead to job modification that will naturally lead to workers returning to normal behaviour rather than the damaged behaviour they exhibit when at work in a dysfunctional, restrictive environment.

Once it is noticed that forcing people to work tends to demotivate them, some organizations turn to systems that use a mixture of external rewards and punishments. You get the reward if you learn how to do as many jobs as possible and you do them in the way that the managers have decided is the best way!

Unfortunately, such an approach systematically weakens people's internal motivation leaving the management to find shiny new ways to keep everyone working at the same pace. It's simpler and more effective to share the goal and free people to decide how to achieve it.

People are happier with choices. We want our work to mean something. Don't you? We can think up our own rewards, our own goals and our own means to achieving them. All we need is freedom to do our best. And it works; just listen to an executive from DuPont who thought that letting workers make their own decisions would be like 'handing the prison over to the inmates':

"Before we had everyone climbing the same ladder. Now we can scale any market change or customer retooling infinitely faster. Everyone is climbing the wall on their own ladder, supporting the same business direction." [28]

Imagine people at work enjoying no limits to the number and nature of rewarding experiences. Think about the business enjoying the benefits of self-renewing, self-regenerating motivation. Gone is the need to entertain or threaten to get people working! The work itself becomes the reward. And in a society where fulfilment is valued above money, it's about time.

Gone is the need to entertain or threaten to get people working!

Let everyone in your organization share the goal, the planning process, the objectives setting, the strategy, and then let them figure out the best way that they can contribute.

Then you have what University of Chicago psychologist, Mihaly Csikszentmihalyi calls 'emergent motivation', motivation that cannot be predicted and comes from the relationship between each person and their work. And this can only happen when work is allowed to become a source of self-expression.

In the words of one union president:

❝I used to come to work so I could get the money to put into the two small street businesses I ran. I just sold the second one because my life feels more integrated now. Now the real me can come to work, have a wild hair of an idea that can make a particular customer really successful and follow everything through as though I were the boss. I actually forget they are not my own personal customers, like at my old shop. I never knew life and work could be the same thing.❞ [29]

Why should work be something that is done to unwilling victims who submit only in return for money? When the work becomes the reward, you get caring that you can't buy. That's how you keep customers. That's how you stop the union/business conflict by understanding that union concerns are not roadblocks. Unshrinking is how you get the 'full-time' employee, the employee who brings his heart and mind to work. Of course, many will respond: but the interests of unions, management and customers are not the same – you cannot just gloss over the conflicts. Our starting point is different. Of course we accept that the interests of different groups are not always the same; the problem is that the myths pretend that they are *always* opposed, as though we were not an inter-dependent species. Most conflict is gratuitous. The fact that an organization is a community does not mean that conflicting demands will never exist within that community. The point is that it is not a machine; the company is not separate from the people. People are all there is. Let us look at our next principle.

PRINCIPLE SEVEN: PEOPLE DO WHAT THEY WANT

There is always room for discretion – always some element of choice. People will not obey wholeheartedly unless they understand why, unless they agree, unless they believe in the rule maker, unless they are on-side. When the rules are not imposed but are instead natural statements of the way that work is done and the way that the organization and its members want it to be done then – and only then – will rules be followed.

No organization is immune from rule breakers. Consider the embarrassment of the CIA when it discovered that its secret service staff and contractors had hacked its networks and set up a secret chat room in which they exchanged 'inappropriate' e-mail and other materials. Only four employees lost their jobs but over 160 participants had taken part undetected over a 20-year period.

So ask yourself. Does the CIA depend on rules or the desire of its people to obey them? Compliance cannot be assumed. Omniscience is not a management trait. They cannot be every-where, watching everything (although look how hard they try with each new piece of technology!) and so they must rely on trust to get the job done legally, and to the satisfaction of customers.

What are rules for anyway? Who says that we need them? How many do we need? What we need are principles. People can govern themselves if they understand and accept principles. Some rules are necessary. Some rules are legally required. But the over-reliance on

People can govern themselves if they understand and accept principles.

rules is damaging and distorts the nature of organizations.

Good managers ignore as many of the rules as they can while still remaining honest, legal, and effective. Good managers do not need to use clock-in systems or timers on the restroom lights to keep their employees working productively.

If the culture and behaviour of the employees has become dishonest then change the culture, change the people, and don't think that the rules will help in the medium and long term. Do not aim to create (or keep) a rules-driven, slave-like organization. Let and encourage people to be what they want to be and to support as far as they can the objectives of the organization. No pressure one way or the other. Reward them to the extent that they want to contribute.

Too often rules stop people thinking. They stop people growing. They provide excuses not to deal with the real world, filled with real people, as it really is.

Just accept that control won't work to achieve positive benefits. (It damages the obedient and compliant while just providing one more distraction to the ineffective and failing completely to control the disenchanted and dishonest slackers!) Once you can get that into your head then you are at last dealing with the world as it is, rather than some concocted world of myth and fantasy where unions and business schools have played for too long.

Does this mean anarchy? Quite the opposite. Anarchy comes in regimented workplaces, where people will go to extraordinary lengths to break unnecessary rules just to assert their free will. A workplace based on trust is a place for grown-up, complete people with families, brains, unfulfilled ambitions and pride.

When a bunch of rules is put before essential principles then the principles risk being obscured, ignored or disfigured. When a business cannot do what it wants to do, what it thinks is smart, even when it is legal and moral, just because of the 'rules' then it has a rules problem.

Think of all those pointless rules. Uniforms and business dress for people who are never seen by the public. Call centre staff uniforms! Why? Life and complexity are beyond the possibilities of a manual or rulebook to legislate. Rushed legislation is bad legislation. Rules often are built up as scar tissue resulting from injury.

> **Rules often are built up as scar tissue resulting from injury.**

Take the issue of employee use of the web as an example. Management is shocked because those 'lazy' employees are using the internet to go to 'non-job related' websites. But at the same time, they want their employees to understand the internet and to have well-developed computers skills. As a recent Forrester report put it:

"The IS department is happy, because the network bandwidth is under control, but even business use of the web has declined. Employees are no longer browsing the web during their lunch breaks. Instead, they have gone back to their old habits — taking 90-minute lunch 'hours' and hanging out in the halls. Productivity is down, and animosity between managers and employees is up." [30]

So often business managers think that people would rather gain the benefits of keeping the rules than the benefits of *not* keeping the rules. Where do we think that rebellion comes from? Where do revolutions come from? Better to feed the Indians than to fight them. The desire to do our own thing. The desire to make a difference.

Consider the recollection of the Russian writer Fyodor Dosto-evsky from his years spent doing forced labour in a prison in Siberia in the 19th century.

"Behind the fortress on the frozen river were two govern-ment barges. They were useless, and had to be broken up so that the timber might not be lost. The timber was itself almost worthless, for firewood can be bought in the town at a nominal price, the whole countryside being covered with forests. The work was simply intended to give us something to do, as was understood on both sides; and accordingly we went to it apathetically. Things were very different when there was a useful job or some definite scheme to be carried out. In that case, although the men themselves derived no profit, they tried to get it done as soon as possible, and took a pride in doing it quickly. But when the labour was a matter of form rather than of necessity, no high-powered effort could be expected." [31]

Here were several hundred prisoners, the bulk of them illiterate and of peasant stock, who received no pay for their work. Yet it mattered to them whether their work was important; whether it helped other people.

The prisoners were under instruction every moment of their waking lives. Their every action was subject to both the instruc-tion and observation of the prison guards. They lived under constant threat of physical punishments, in the form of beatings, for any transgression. If they tried to escape they were likely to be shot. Despite this they took every opportunity to break rules if there was not a rational purpose for them.

It is the concept of a better world, perhaps just a slightly better world, that gives meaning and fulfilment to people's work. In conventional

Life doesn't follow the zero sum theories of Adam Smith and Karl Marx.

thinking the notions of profit making and helping people are taken to be each other's opposites. Yet in the real world many grasping people set on making their millions fail, while benevolent institutions end up being accidentally profitable. Life doesn't follow the zero sum theories of Adam Smith and Karl Marx.

Keep
the faith

This is going to sound evangelical, but please stay with us. Once we had fully absorbed the meaning of the originally sketchy principles that we essayed, everything became clearer. There is a link between the education policy that goes wrong, the company merger that fails, the executives who neglect their families, the child who gets labelled 'stupid', the boss who prevents staff from learning. These are all symptoms of the myths that shrink us.

Most of the people failing do not want to; most of those causing pain would rather do good. We have been brought up to believe that there is always a trade-off or a choice between doing that which is good and that which leads to success. Such an assumption is wrong, and this is a tremendously liberating realization. One can quickly see that it does not only apply to the matters of management and education that we have concentrated on here. It has implications for trade, for politics and for economic development. You have probably thought of some already.

We have only just begun the inquiry. Do join us.

Remember, it doesn't have to be this way.

www.unshrinkthepeople.com

Unshrink notes

There's a lot to unshrink

1 'John Karas, a Lockheed Martin vice president, insists both sides have done everything possible to avoid a launch-day disaster. But he notes: 'Until you fly, you never know, and I'm as superstitious as the next guy.' With that, he knocks on wood. More than once.

2 The Holmes-Rahe scale, which measures the increasing complexity of life, has calculated that life today is on average 44 per cent more difficult than 30 years ago.

3 Byrne, J. A. (1999) *Chainsaw: The Notorious Career of Al Dunlap in the Era of Profit-at-any-Price.* Harper Business.

1 Unshrink yourself

1 'How Do You Know Who You Can Trust?' by Leslie. www.teenwire.com/warehouse/articles/wh_1998201p028.asp

Whenever there's a lecture at school, or a TV show about a sensitive subject like sex or drugs, at the end the lecturers always say you should 'seek out a relative, a teacher, a clergyman or an adult you trust' if you have more questions. But 'Who do I trust?' is a tough question to answer. Eventually there comes a time when talking to your friends your own age isn't enough. Talking to your parents might seem scary and so you need to find someone to confide in who will keep your best interests at heart.

I used the trial and error method, and ultimately found Mr and Mrs Allen. I used to babysit for their kids. I chose them because they treated me — well, not exactly like an adult — but they demonstrated in both word and deed (leaving me in charge of their children) that they had faith in me. They seemed to genuinely like me and they were interested in the part of my life that went on when I wasn't watching their boys. More importantly, they were the adult version of who I hoped to be one day: hip, smart, educated, unpretentious and warm. They were a little different from everyone else in my homogeneous neighborhood and unapologetic about it. They were secure people. Here's my list for deciding who to trust:

- Do they have anything to lose or gain by your decisions?
- Do they demonstrate a genuine interest in more than one aspect of your life?
- Do you feel they respect you for who you already are? (This will translate into respect for the person you are becoming.)
- Do you respect them?
- Do they live in a way you aspire to?
- Do they have values similar to yours?
- Do they have their act together, or are they constantly fixing messes?
- Do they have time for you, or at least consistently make time for you?
- Does your gut feeling say you can trust them?
- Finally, ask yourself is this someone you genuinely like, or is it just someone you want to like you? If you're eager to have the person like you, they may not make the best

mentor because you'll be tempted to go against your instincts to please them. Or, even more likely, you may not make a clear judgement about whether they're going to respect you as a person or not.

2 Lajis, R. H. (1966) *The History of Drug Abuse in Sports*. National Poison Centre, Malaysia.
Some athletes are happy to use beta-adrenoceptor blockers and beta-adrenoceptor agonists, calcium-channel blockers, blood doping diuretics, growth hormone and growth hormone stimulants, non-steroidal anti-inflammatory drugs, iron, theophylline and in some situations, vitamins.

3 www.novastor.com/nova_store/info/careers.html (2001) Job Code HR-SA1.

4 Pfeffer, J. (2001) *Business and the Spirit*, Research Paper no. 1713. Stanford University Research Paper Series.

5 Bill Moushey, investigative reporter for the *Pittsburgh Post-Gazette* (www.post-gazette.com).

6 Quoted by Robert Merkle, whom President Ronald Reagan appointed US Attorney for the Middle District of Florida, serving from 1982 to 1988, in 'Out of Control', by Bill Moushey, *Post-Gazette* Staff Writer, 22 November 1998.

7 Tim Johnson, Manager of the Toronto Blue Jays in 1998.

8 Shields, D. (2000) 'Bob Knight, c'est moi', 27 September, Salon.com.

9 http://members.aol.com/rmkgeneral/ Just listen to the recording of Bob Knight at work!

10 Williams, D. (1998) 'Leadership for the 21st Century', Hay Group report; see also Golman, D. *et al* (2001) 'Primal Leader-

ship: the Hidden Driver of Great Performance', *Harvard Business Review*, December.

11 Updated: Monday 20 April 1998 at 23:18 CDT 'Star athletes are models — not parents, Aikman says' by Mede Nix Star-Telegram Dallas bureau.

12 King, S. (2000) *On Writing: A Memoir of the Craft*, Hodder & Stoughton.

13 From an interview by Philip Whiteley in 1991 with a general practitioner in Managua.

14 Howard, K. (1999) 'Do brain cells regenerate?', *Princeton Weekly Bulletin*, 5 April.

15 'Running boosts number of brain cells according to new Salk study', 22 February 1999. The Salk Institute for Biological Studies, La Jolla, California, USA.

16 Gardner, H. (2000) *Intelligence Reframed: Multiple Intelligences for the 21st Century*. Basic Books.

17 Zeichner (1995) states the importance of teachers and prospective teachers having high expectations for all students. The first element common to effective teachers in urban schools is the belief that all students can be successful learners and the communication of this belief to students (Delpit, 1988; Lucas, Henze, & Donato, 1990; Quality Education for Minorities Project, 1990). These teachers have a personal commitment to helping all students achieve success and truly believe that they can make a difference in their students' achievement (Hodge, 1990). Winfield (1986) distinguishes between teachers who assume responsibility for their students' learning and those who shift responsibility, when students fail, to factors such as school bureaucracies, parents and

communities. Despite evidence to the contrary, many students in teacher education institutions continue to cling to the belief that some students cannot learn, and so they hold low expectations for them (Goodlad, 1990).

18 See the Dyslexia Research Institute website for research papers and findings (www.dyslexia–add.org).

19 'Those who can do, those who can't, bully' (www.successunlimited.co.uk/bully).

20 *Analysis*, BBC Radio 4, 'Forgiveness', 23 December 1999.

21 Pfeffer, J. (1994) *Competitive Advantage Through People.* Harvard Business Press.

22 Smith, C. (1999) *The Mail & Guardian*, 24 December, South Africa.

23 Idem.

24 Salon.com, 18 November 1999.

25 That disturbing observation comes from Suzanne Braun Levine, formerly editor of *Ms* magazine and the *Columbia Journalism Review*. Levine, who lives in New York, is author of *Father Courage: What Happens When Men Put Family First* (2000). Harcourt.

26 www.fitnessandfreebies.com/fitness/overtrain.html

27 www.actu.asn.au/archive/hottopic/overload/ National Campaign on Work Overload 9–13 November 1998, 'Say no to work overload'.

28 Figures from 1997. Taken from 'Myths about work-related diseases' in *The Burden of Occupational Illness*, World Health Organization, 8 June 1999.

29 www.freedomtocare.org

30 Lyman, R. (1999) 'A Tobacco Whistle-Blower's Life is Transformed', *New York Times*, 15 October.

31 Temple, P. 'Your sins will find you out', http://bsstudents uce.ac.uk/lecturers/Bob%20Curry/Personal%20Portfolio%20 Planning/ARTICLES/Ethics.htm

32 *Financial Times*, 15 July 2001.

33 See 31.

34 Simon, H. B. (1999) 'Can work kill?', *Scientific American*, June.

35 Cryer, B. (1996) 'Neutralizing workplace stress: the physiology of human performance and organizational effectiveness', presented at Psychological Difficulties in the Workplace, the Center for Professional Learning, Toronto, Canada, 12 June 1996.

36 Flyvbjerg, B. (2001) *Making Social Science Matter*. Cambridge University Press.

37 *Analysis*, BBC Radio 4, 'Plain Speaking', 28 October 1999, Dr Anthony Grayling, a lecturer in philosophy at Birkbeck College, London.

38 'Busy parents bid goodnight to bedtime stories' (2000) *The Times*, 2 November.

39 Brewer, E. H. (1999) *Hindered by unhappiness – a review of primary school interventions to support children who cause concern*. Coram Family. London.

40 'To dot.com or not to dot.com', Livelyhood, compiled by Angela Morgenstern for the Working Group, KQED TV, www.pbs.org/livelyhood/workday/dotcom/ somedotcommers.html

41 From ****(anonymous) the overachiever, an anonymous rant on whywork.og

42 '*The management agenda*' (2001) Research paper, Roffey Park Institute.

2 Unshrink others

1 Pfeffer, J. (1994) *Competitive Advantage Through People*. Harvard Business School Press.

2 Major, T. (2001) 'Germany's leadership by committee faces extinction', *Financial Times*, 28 November.

3 Mintzberg, H. and Lampel J. (2001) 'MBAs as CEOs' www.henrymintzberg.com

4 From an interview Philip Whiteley carried out with Chris Grant.

5 Dreyfus, H. and Dreyfus, S. (1996) *Mind Over Machine*. New York Free Press; and Flyvbjerg B, (2001) *Making Social Science Matter*. Cambridge University Press.

6 McKay, R. (1999) 'Got more? Give more', *Council on Foundations Magazine*.

There is more need for philanthropy than ever before. The rising tide of the US economy clearly is lifting more yachts than dinghies. New figures from the Congressional Budget Office reveal that the gap between rich and poor in this country is the widest in history, having doubled since 1977. Despite record returns of the Dow and other markets, a report by the US Conference of Mayors shows that homelessness is rising at its fastest pace in five years. The same study shows that the percentage of homeless families with children has jumped one-quarter since 1985. Nationally, almost 14 per cent of Americans — and nearly 21 per cent of children — live in poverty.

Government cutbacks, corporate downsizing and consolidation, welfare reform and other factors have put added pressure on middle- and low-income people, even as foundation assets swell. Philanthropy's minimum giving rate of 5 per cent cannot be characterized as 'stepping up to the plate' to meet these growing needs.

Philanthropy can do more to meet that need. With gales of economic change swirling around us, it is mystifying why so much of the philanthropic world is attempting to proceed as if nothing is happening. The *Washington Post* reported that although foundations had $56 billion more to work with in 1998 than 1997, 'they stuck close to the minimum required payout' of 5 per cent. The Mehrling study shows that foundation payout actually declined from 8 per cent in 1981 to below 5 per cent in 1997— during a period described by most observers as flush for foundations.

The DeMarche study concludes that a hypothetical foundation could have paid out as much as 6.5 per cent over the past 20 years and still seen its portfolio grow 23.9 per cent. Nevertheless, DeMarche discourages foundations from doing just that, falling back on its familiar counter-intuitive conclusion that 'lower initial spending results in higher aggregate spending over time' (again, without addressing the dramatic impact new giving has had).

The McKay Foundation's focus is on building the community of grantees while being financially responsible.

'We support organizing, advocacy and the efforts of communities who organize on their own behalf to create a more just society. We employ community strategies to work for equality, economic development and empowerment. Our giving includes addressing the struggle of the homeless, environmental degradation and women's rights.

'McKay works closely with its investment managers not only so that we are financially responsible, but so that our values shine through the numbers. Consequently, the mission of our foundation is reflected both in the quality of our giving and in the fact that our foundation has averaged a 17 per cent payout rate. As one of 35,000 family-led foundations existing today, we continue to grow – even with a payout rate 3.5 times the required amount.'

NNG's '1% More for Democracy' campaign, which calls for 1 per cent in grants to go towards resolving hunger, homelessness, poverty, inequality and other social needs, seems a more rational benchmark than holding on to the status quo. It also seems an effective way to keep Congress from eventually mandating a higher payout rate and taking away our choice of doing so.

Ultimately, foundation directors should consult not only DeMarche Associates, Goldman Sachs Assets Management and other investment houses when determining their payout, but programme directors, grantees and their own hearts. The purpose of philanthropy, after all, is to make grants that will enhance our lives now and build a better world, not simply increase our asset base for hypothetical battles in the future. We can fight today's battles and tomorrow's, but only by giving our maximum, not our minimum, effort.

7 'We are not waiting, necessarily, to die to do good things ...The starting point for that is to change the real definition of 'legacy' from doing something at the time that you have died to doing good deeds while you are alive. We are trying to teach people, to help them see how they can make a difference, and think of dream projects during their lifetime as being their best legacy.' Claude Rosenberg, Founder & Chairman, New Tithing Group (1998).

8 In order to tap this vast source of wealth, Paul Schervish, Director of the Social Welfare Institute at Boston College, asserted that it's essential to understand what he calls 'the new physics of philanthropy'. The 'old physics,' he added, revolved around a 'scolding model'. The wealthy were, in effect, scolded for having money. They were told they weren't giving enough, at the right time, to the right causes, and in the right way. The 'new physics', in contrast, revolves around the inclination of donors to identify with a cause. It asks people, Schervish said: 'Is there something you want to do that attends to the care of others, that you can do better when you are choosing the way, and the methods, and the purposes, and that expresses your gratitude, brings you satisfaction, and fulfills your self?' Help the very rich see that they and their heirs cannot possibly consume all of their growing wealth. According to Paul Schervish: 'That [recognition] provides ... not a mandate for them to give to charity, but an opportunity to do so.'

9 Lower-income donors have become increasingly generous. In 1995, Americans with annual incomes below $10,000 donated

4.3 per cent of their household incomes. Conversely, those in the $75,000 to $99,000 bracket gave only 1.8 per cent of their household income. Reported in PBS Newshour Online Forum (1999).

10 Botham, I. (1994) *Don't Tell Kath, Botham: My Autobiography*. Collins Willow.

11 From and interview with Sir Robin Saxby conducted by Philip Whiteley.

12 Galeano, E. (1978) *Open Veins of Latin America (Las Venas Abiertas de America Latina)*, additional chapter in 2nd edition, Sigolo Veintiuno Editores

13 Kallio, J. *et al.* (1999) 'Drivers and tracers of business p rocess changes', *Journal of Strategic Information Systems*, 8: 125142.

14 Jeremy Bell, an IT configuration systems specialist in the UK, recalls in an interview with Philip Whiteley, how his colleagues were made redundant once at a software company employing 300 people. December 2001.

3 Unshrink your business

1 Crainer, S, (2000) *The Management Century*. Booze-Allen & Hamilton.

2 Kay, J. (1999) 'Rough Counting', *Analysis*, Radio 4, 4 November. Whether he created the term or is merely popularising it is not quite clear. http://news.bbc.co.uk/hi/english/static/audio-video/ programmes/analysis/tanscripts/rough/txt

3 Bowe, C. (1999) Executive Chairperson of Save and Prosper, and former head of the Personal Investment Authority. 'Rough Counting', *Analysis*, Radio 4, 4 November. http://news.

bbc.co.uk/hi/english/static/audio-video/programmes/
analysis/tanscripts/rough/txt

4 Kellaway, L. (2001) 'Games for executives', *Financial Times*, 4
March.

5 http://web.lexis-nexis.com/more/worldatwork/19149/
6856742/1

6 *Unlocking Shareholder Value: The Keys to Success*, (1999)
KPMG; see also *Mergers: Tending to be Short on Bliss*, FT
Life Sciences http://specials.ft.com/ln/ftsurveys/q4b62.htm

7 Champy, J. (1995) *Re-Engineering Management.* Harper
Business, New York; see also Webster, D. Black, M. (1997)
*Business Process Re-Engineering: A Case Study of a Devel-
opmental Approach*, Centre for Labour Market Studies.
www.clms.le.ac.uk/WWW/publications/wkpapers/working_p
aperNo21.pdf

8 Taylor III, A. (2001) 'Jacques Nasser — crunch time for Jac',
Fortune magazine, 25 June.

9 http://web.lexis-nexis.com/more/worldatwork/19149/
6856742/1

10 Gratton *et al.* (1997) *Strategic Human Resource Management.* Oxford University Press.

11 Patterson, M. *et al.* (1997) *Impact of People Management
Practices on Business Performance.* Chartered Institute of
Personnel & Development.

12 www.rci.rutgers.edu/~huselid/

13 *Watson Wyatt's Human Capital Index.* The international consultancy Watson Wyatt has completed two thorough surveys
of human resources practices at major companies – one in
North America and one in Europe.

14 www.watsonwyatt.com

15 www.gallupjournal.com/GMJarchive/issue1/2001315i.asp

16 See 6.

17 www.gallupjournal.com/GMJarchive/issue1/2001315i.asp

18 To learn more about intellectual capital, go to www.intellectualcapital.se, set up by Leif Edvinsson. Another good starting point is an article in *Fast Company*, January/February 2000, featuring an interview with Baruch Lev, to be found at www.fastcompany.com/online/31/lev.html

19 Donnelly, G. 'Recruiting, retention and returns', *CFO* magazine, March 2000.

20 Keynes, J. M. (1972) *General theory of Employment, Interest and Money*. Harcourt.

21 Marx, K. (1867) *Das Kapital* I.

22 These observations are based on a two-week tour of the Cuban health service made in 1993 by Philip Whiteley.

23 From an interview with Jon Sparkes conducted by Philip Whiteley.

24 From an interview with Brad Hill conducted by Philip Whiteley.

25 Idem.

26 B Mod is based on the work of B.F. Skinner who argues that behaviour is a function of its consequences rather than a function of internal needs and motives. Of course IT IS BOTH! It is yet another artificially conflicting position taken to found a new school of thinking rather than to unshrink the people.

27 *Organizational Behaviour* (2000) FT Knowledge.

28 *Myths of High Performance Work Systems Date*, de diffusion 21 October 1999 #2: Regenerative Work Designs.

29 Sanford, C. 'Regenerative business practices', in *At Work: Stories for Tomorrow's Workplace.* Berrett-Koehler Publishers.

30 Forrester Research (2001). E-mail newsletter about staff internet usage.

31 Dostoevsky, F. (1962) *The House of the Dead.* JM Dent & Sons.

Other books by Max McKeown:

Why They Don't Buy
make your online customer experience work

Financial Times Prentice Hall 2002
ISBN: 0 273 65674 0

If you want to have online customers, then online customers must want to have your online buying experience. So, what do you need to do in order to build a profitable, differentiated and world-beating customer experience online?

It's not enough to be on the web and it's not enough to build a great site – however functional or funky. You have to meet and exceed every expectation of the new e-customer. This is the science of selling online. In *Why they Don't Buy*, online customer guru Max McKeown delivers a complete programme for building the ultimate online customer experience.

E-customer
customers just got faster and smarter – catch up

Financial Times Prentice Hall 2001
ISBN: 0 273 65020 3

"The e-customer does not care about traditional boundaries between products, organisations, or departments. The e-customer wants an improved life-style. He will remain loyal to the source of simplicity, care, and good value." **Max McKeown**